# Friends and Lovers
# in the College Years

*Formulated by the Committee on the College Student
Group for the Advancement of Psychiatry*

## Mental Health Materials Center
30 E. 29th Street, New York, N.Y. 10016

**Library of Congress Cataloging in Publication Data**

Group for the Advancement of Psychiatry. Committee on the College Student.
  Friends and lovers.

  (Publication; v. 11, no. 115)
    1. College students—Psychology. 2. College student orientation. I. Title. II.
Series: Publication (Group for the Advancement of Psychiatry); no. 11.
LB3609.G76   1983                          378'.198                          83-8119
ISBN 0-910958-20-3

*May, 1983, Volume XI, Publication No. 115*

*This is the ninth and final number in a series of GAP publication comprising Volume XI.*

*Manufactured in the United States of America.*

# TABLE OF CONTENTS

# STATEMENT OF PURPOSE

THE GROUP FOR THE ADVANCEMENT OF PSYCHIATRY has a membership of approximately 300 psychiatrists, most of whom are organized in the form of a number of working committees. These committees direct their efforts toward the study of various aspects of psychiatry and the application of this knowledge to the fields of mental health and human relations.

Collaboration with specialists in other disciplines has been and is one of GAP's working principles. Since the formation of GAP in 1946 its members have worked closely with such other specialists as anthropologists, biologists, economists, statisticians, educators, lawyers, nurses, psychologists, sociologists, social workers, and experts in mass communication, philosophy, and semantics. GAP envisages a continuing program of work according to the following aims:

1.  To collect and appraise significant data in the fields of psychiatry, mental health, and human relations

2.  To reevaluate old concepts and to develop and test new ones

3.  To apply the knowledge thus obtained for the promotion of mental health and good human relations.

GAP is an independent group, and its reports represent the composite findings and opinions of its members only, guided by its many consultants.

*Friends and Lovers in the College Years* was formulated by the Committee on the College Student, which acknowledges on page xi the participation of others in the preparation of this report.

The members of this committee are listed below. The following pages list the members of the other GAP committees as well as additional membership categories and current and past officers of GAP.

COMMITTEE ON THE COLLEGE STUDENT

*Malkah Tolpin Notman, Brookline, Mass.,
   Chairperson
Robert L. Arnstein, Hamden, Conn.
Varda Peller Ganz Backus, LaJolla, Calif.
Myron B. Liptzin, Chapel Hill, N.C.
Gloria Onque, Pittsburgh, Pa.
Elizabeth Aub Reid, Cambridge, Mass.
*Kent Robinson, Towson, Md.
Earle Silber, Chevy Chase, Md.


COMMITTEE ON AGING

Charles M. Gaitz, Houston, Tex., Chairperson
Gene D. Cohen, Rockville, Md.
Lawrence F. Greenleigh, Los Angeles, Calif.
Maurice E. Linden, Philadelphia, Pa.
Robert J. Nathan, Philadelphia, Pa.
Eric Pfeiffer, Denver, Co.
George H. Pollock, Chicago, Ill.
Harvey L. Ruben, New Haven, Conn.
F. Conyers Thompson, Jr., Atlanta, Ga.
Prescott W. Thompson, San Jose, Calif.


COMMITTEE ON ADOLESCENCE

Warren J. Gadpaille, Englewood, Colo.,
   Chairperson
Ian A. Canino, New York, N.Y.
Harrison P. Eddy, New York, N.Y.
Sherman C. Feinstein, Highland Park, Ill.
Michael Kalogerakis, New York, N.Y.
Clarice J. Kestenbaum, New York, N.Y.
Derek Miller, Chicago, Ill.
Silvio J. Onesti, Jr., Belmont, Mass.

---

* During the formulation of this report,
   Dr. Notman served as chairperson of this
   committee. The current chairperson is Dr.
   Robinson.

COMMITTEE ON CHILD PSYCHIATRY

John F. McDermott, Jr., Honolulu, Hawaii,
   Chairperson
Paul L. Adams, Louisville, Ky.
James M. Bell, Canaan, N.Y.
Harlow Donald Dunton, New York, N.Y.
Joseph Fischoff, Detroit, Mich.
Joseph M. Green, Madison, Wis.
John Schowalter, New Haven, Conn.
Theodore Shapiro, New York, N.Y.
Peter Tanguay, Los Angeles, Calif.
Lenore F. C. Terr, San Francisco, Calif.


COMMITTEE ON CULTURAL PSYCHIATRY

Andrea K. Delgado, New York, N.Y.,
   Chairperson
Edward F. Foulks, Philadelphia, Pa.
Ezra E. H. Griffith, New Haven, Conn.
Pedro Ruiz, Houston, Tex.
John P. Spiegel, Waltham, Mass.
Ronald M. Wintrob, Farmington, Conn.
Joseph Yamamoto, Los Angeles, Calif.


COMMITTEE ON THE FAMILY

Henry U. Grunebaum, Cambridge, Mass.,
   Chairperson
W. Robert Beavers, Dallas, Tex.
Ellen M. Berman, Merion, Pa.
Lee Combrinck-Graham, Philadelphia, Pa.
Ira D. Glick, New York, N.Y.
Frederick Gottlieb, Los Angeles, Calif.
Charles A. Malone, Cleveland, Ohio
Joseph Satten, San Francisco, Calif.


COMMITTEE ON GOVERNMENTAL AGENCIES

William W. Van Stone, Palo Alto, Calif.,
   Chairperson,
James P. Cattell, Monterey, Mass.
Sidney S. Goldensohn, New York, N.Y.
Naomi Heller, Washington, D.C.
Roger Peele, Washington, D.C.

# COMMITTEE ACKNOWLEDGEMENTS

During the preparation of this report, two GAP members, no longer serving on this committee contributed significantly to the deliberations leading to its final version. They were Harrison P. Eddy, III, who has since its completion, joined the Committee on Adolescence, and Tom G. Stauffer who transferred to contributing status. The Committee also wishes to express its appreciation to the help it received in formulating its findings and observations to the four Ginsburg Fellows who were assigned to it during the period FRIENDS AND LOVERS IN THE COLLEGE YEARS was in the making. They were: Robert L. Friend, Elton Hurst, Frank Kirchner, and Leslie Lopato.

Malkah T. Notman, Chairperson
*Committee on the College Student*

# Preamble

"The train started with a sudden crunching...He had embarked, and the quick plunge into the darkness of the long tunnel had, to his keenly sentimental imagination, something of the dark transition from one world into another. Behind with the known and the accomplished; ahead the coming of man's estate and man's freedom. He was his own master at last, free to go and to come, free to venture and to experience, free to know that strange, guarded mystery—life—and free, knowing it, to choose from among it many ways.

"Behind him remained the city, suddenly hushed. He was on the campus, the Brick Row at his left;...Somewhere there in the great protecting embrace of these walls were the friends that should be his, that should pass with him through those wonderful years of happiness and good fellowship that were coming."*

So was this young man anticipating his college experience over seventy years ago. Much has changed, but the importance of relationships in these years has remained.

---

*Stover at Yale, Owen Johnson Collier Books, New York, 1968. Originally published by Frederick A. Stokes Co., 1912.

# INTRODUCTION

Although through history there have been occasional contented hermits, it is generally accepted that human beings need and want relationships with other human beings. The first relationship, the parent-infant relationship at birth, is essential to survival, and successive relationships serve a variety of functions, ranging from physical and psychological nurturance and protection to companionship, sexual gratification, emotional support, and expression of aggressive and self-assertive needs. An individual's physical and emotional maturation cannot proceed without relationships, which are used, both consciously and unconsciously, in the service of development.

Compared with a generation ago, there seems to be a wider range of socially accepted relationships prevalent in late adolescence and early adulthood. There are long-term committed sexual relationships not necessarily leading to marriage (e.g., couples living together for significant periods of time); there are a variety of friendships with deep emotional content including nonsexualized friendships between men and women; and there are relationships between men and women which involve new conventions and new definitions of appropriate sex roles. The extent, the meaning, and the implications of these relationships have been questioned. Are the changes more apparent than real? Will the patterns change in time? What psychological and social functions do they serve?

Whether in old forms or new, relationships are crucial for development. They are especially important in the college years, and much of the personal and emotional growth of this period is intimately connected with the character and vicissitudes of a student's relationships with other students, faculty, family, and a variety of others. This report will discuss the forms and functions of these relationships and how they influence development in the late adolescent-young adult period. Although all adolescents must move into adulthood, those who go to college experience these relationships in an environment offering special intellectual, social, and emotional stimuli and during a period in which full assumption of adult social roles and responsibilities is postponed.

The college experience is obviously not uniform, for colleges themselves are varied. Furthermore, the situation of a student at a residential college away from the parental home clearly differs from that of the student who attends college while living at home. Nevertheless, similarities exist in the college experience because there is the postponement of commitment to adult goals and adult life styles and a consequent blurring of the transition from adolescence to adulthood. Although colleges currently may include a significant number of older students, this report will focus on students who attend college at the more traditional ages of seventeen to twenty-three.

In college there is explicit emphasis on learning, intellectual activity, and creative thought. Because of this academic emphasis, social and emotional development—specifically the importance of relationships—is often overlooked or relegated to the background. In fact, however, students form and learn from relationships which comprise an "unacknowledged curriculum." This "curriculum" is complex: the impact and character of relationships can hinder or advance an individual's development; the state of development can strongly influence the quality of, and capacity for relationships; and there is a likely interaction between intellectual and emotional growth. Relationships as they affect development will be considered against the back-drop of the current era of rapid social change with its altered patterns of

life and expectations. Because an individual's particular upbring-
ing and prior developmental experience influence ways of
relating, relationships with family will also be considered as they
affect the developmental tasks specific to late adolescence and
early adulthood. An attempt will be made to identify those
elements of college life and those institutional policies which
facilitate more satisfying relationships, as well as some of the
obstacles to satisfactory relationships created by current aspects of
the campus environment.

# 1
## SOCIAL CHANGE AND RELATIONSHIPS

A variety of forces in American society have recently created changes in patterns of relationship as well as in the way these patterns are regarded and understood. The development of psychoanalytic theory and other scientific observations in the early part of the century did much to unsettle many previously accepted theories about both hierarchical and peer relationships, particularly in relation to sexual and non-sexual elements. Freud, in his delineation of psychosexual development, broadened the concept of "sexual" beyond adult, genital responses to include positive affectional feelings as well as unconscious sensual responses from infancy on.[1] He also postulated that in the course of early development every child has an eroticized relationship with one or both parents, although the erotic component can be largely unconscious. These findings tended to blur the prior sharp distinctions between eroticized and non-eroticized relationships. Furthermore, Freud described the bisexual potential within individuals and suggested that homosexual impulses and heterosexual impulses were not so unlike in psychic origin as had been previously believed, representing a difference in choice of object rather than an entirely separate sexual configuration.[2]

While new developments in psychological theory were occurring, major changes were taking place in social patterns. During the first half of the century, patterns remaining from the Victorian era predominated although there were significant

1

changes in the post-World War I era. A child would usually associate primarily with members of the same sex during the elementary school period, even though primary school was almost always coeducational, and a certain amount of teasing about "girlfriends" and "boyfriends" might occur. At puberty, when genital sexual impulses became stronger and more clearly defined there were intermittent experimental forays in the direction of eroticized relationships. These might be either exclusively emotional, or sexual, or a combination of the two. One relationship would eventually become more important erotically and become semi-permanent (e.g., going steady); in time, this might lead to the formal, permanent relationship of marriage. In some social sub-groups the "courting" routine was precisely defined, but in most social groups in the United States a moderate amount of freedom existed in the choice of partner and the nature of the courting. Sometimes patterns of monogamous relationships predominated even in the courting. In the other setting, dating a number of girls or boys was important. Friendships, however, remained primarily limited to one's own sex.

In the aftermath of World War II, the pace of change accelerated, becoming particularly rapid in the last twenty years. Major questions have been raised about the traditional definition of male-female relationships. What was once considered "inherent" in the nature of a man and a woman is now recognized to be heavily influenced by socialization and sex role definitions.* The characteristics and consequences of being male or female, i.e,, those aspects of masculinity and feminity which were once considered "natural" and inevitable, are being challenged and redefined. There is some evidence, based on cross-cultural studies, that the tendency for preadolescent children to associate in same sex groups occurs because of innate psychological factors and is

---

* Although gender role has been defined technically as the most accurate term to use, popular usage still frequently adheres to "sex role" and we have chosen this term interchangeably with "gender role" in this discussion.

independent of sociological factors. These patterns, whether innate or not, are reinforced by sex-role stereotyping constraints which make a child of one set feel it is socially inappropriate to participate in the games and activities of the other. Many activities such as certain sports which were previously considered all male have recently been broadened to include both males and females, and consequently preadolescent social groups are currently less rigidly single sex.

Strongly stimulated by the women's movement, definitions of sex roles in the family and work are changing dramatically. Economic pressures have affected traditional patterns by forcing the entry of large numbers of women into the work force. This has been made more feasible by smaller families and by labor-saving devices which have reduced the time necessary for housekeeping and food preparation. The population explosion and concerns which have been raised about overpopulation have led to the awareness that many accepted social patterns were maintained to further procreation. When procreation is no longer so valued, other by-products of these social patterns become open to question, e.g., pressure to early marriage. Improved methods of contraception and the decrease in infant mortality have significantly influenced the birth rate. Currently, the number of pregnancies necessary to achieve a family's desired number of living children is considerably reduced. Increased social and geographical mobility and an increased divorce rate have contributed to the fragmenting of family and social ties. Conversely, the lengthened life span has increased the likelihood of long marriages with a potential divergence of partners' needs, which, in turn, may strain the marriage in ways that were rare in the Victorian period. Fidelity and sexual monogamy had quite a different meaning when it was expected that one partner would die in middle age, and marriage lasted much less than the fifty or sixty years likely at present.[3] Now, the post-parental years may be of long duration and may require adaptation to a relationship that is no longer primarily based on providing and caring for children.

Attitudes toward sexuality and sexual experience have also undergone changes. Research findings have explicated many psychological details of male and female sexuality and dispelled longstanding popular myths. Sexual mores have changed; there have even been biological changes, e.g., menstruation occurs at an earlier age due to widespread improvement in nutrition. Increased social tolerance of overt sexuality and consciousness of human sexual needs have led to greater openness about sexual behavior. Barriers against sexual experimentation have decreased, and both men and women have greater expectations for sexual satisfaction. The basis for the taboo on homosexual behavior has been reexamined as has the whole concept of "normality" in sexual behavior. These changes have led to a flood of sexual discussion in the media so that explicit sexuality is part of the public world to which the late adolescent is exposed. This differs greatly from even a generation ago when adolescent knowledge came primarily from surreptitious, and often highly inaccurate, peer discussion.

Although some of these patterns have had counterparts in past historical periods, they represent a significant shift from those of the last century.

It is difficult to predict which of these changes will be longlasting or how current trends will evolve. Women now slightly outnumber men in college enrollment and have greatly increased career aspirations. Many of these women are planning to establish a career first and bear children later. There has been an increase in first pregnancies after age thirty. Since a woman must have her children within a certain age period, she is under specific time constraints that do not affect a man, and young women planning careers are often confused as to how to reconcile conflicting goals and priorities. Thus, phases of male and female adult development have different timetables, and they influence career development in a manner that may require more complex mutual adaptation than has been previously recognized and acknowledged.

These changes, most of which have occurred in the past two decades, present some unique problems for the current generation of college students who are attempting to become educated and to prepare for life ahead.

Furthermore, the uncertain nature of the future world complicates the developmental tasks to be completed in the transition to adulthood. There are frequent predictions of disaster in a number of forms: overpopulation, economic catastrophes, environmental pollution, energy shortages, threats of military operations, as well as the remote but clear-cut possibility of total annihilation as a result of nuclear warfare. Current economic as well as other problems make past American optimism less plausible. If one assumes that the future is, at best, unpredictable, and, at worst, nonexistent, very long-range planning becomes problematic. As a result, short, as opposed to long-term, commitments may seem more desirable, although some people cling to each other in the face of a threatening world. The psychological supports available for facing an uncertain future are not strong. One must be able to tolerate considerable ambiguity, uncertainty, and anxiety for which no one, let alone an adolescent, is well equipped.

Many are postponing marriage, and, the current generation at least, is having and planning to have fewer children. Traditional family patterns may also seem problematic because increasingly women's expectations include a career as an important ingredient. Some adolescents are disillusioned about marriage as a result of observing their parents' dissatisfaction and the prevalence of divorce. For all these reasons, many students question the viability of the traditional family pattern and search for new modes of relationships that fit more closely into their observations of, and feelings about, the world they see around them. This does not mean that they are necessarily engaging in conscious, thoughtful, purposeful planning about relationships. However, discussion of alternatives is common, and choices are made on the basis of both conscious and unconscious influences.

Thus, most individuals once expected that they would marry

and that the marriage would be stable and lasting. No longer is this felt to be inevitable, and having children as part of the "natural" fulfillment of marriage and the expression of feminine and masculine roles is similarly questioned. If both the man and the woman are economically self-supporting and there are to be no children, marriage is less obligatory, and the character of the commitment to a partner can remain ambiguous. Despite these apparent trends, it should be noted that it is not clear which changes with regard to marriage and family will endure, and which are part of a phasic process that may reverse itself. For example, there is already some suggestion that the trend to fewer expected children is reversing when compared with a decade ago.[4]

People respond to the anxiety caused by contemplating an ambiguous future in various ways; some are conscious, some less so. Some try to find security through an increased emphasis on dependable and safe life styles. After the campus turmoil of the 1960's, the current push toward professionalism may be a response to the anxious uncertainty that seems to result from the current economic realities of job scarcity and mounting inflation. Others may turn to religion or neo-conservative solutions. Still others may respond to this anxiety by greater experimentation with relationships and careers.

Exploring various kinds of relationships has always been characteristic of late adolescent development. It serves the positive function of helping individuals discover the possibilities in relationships, as well as supporting their emotional flexibility and adaptiveness. In the current context of changing values and expectations, adolescent experimentation may range over a greater breadth of possibilities than previously. However, the diminished rigidity of social roles, while providing greater choice, may also constitute a burden because each individual must arrive at his or her own particular code of behavior and style of living with less help from social conventions.

The lack of stable conventions creates further difficulty in regard to the developmental function of relationships. Ordinarily, progression from childhood to adulthood would draw on patterns incorporated in childhood from parents and other adult models. Although personality development does indeed depend on identification with parents, the social changes already described require more complex adaptations than may be available from parental models. Many of the considerations, choices, pressures, and rules of behavior that face individuals of college age are very different from those of their parents' world so that it is difficult to use parents as models in the way that would be possible in a more stable social environment. The problem, thus, is not only learning to establish and develop expectable life patterns, but also to be prepared to adapt and to change these expectations.

# 2
## DEVELOPMENTAL THEORY

Janet came to a competitive, prestigious college with considerable anxiety about how she would fit in and whether she would be able to perform academically and find friends in this rarified atmosphere. She had not really dated in high school; social events had occurred mostly in groups and she spent considerable time studying.

The first few months were tense as the students came to know each other and to classify each other in relation to performance. After the first semester, Janet felt relieved. She realized that although it would be a struggle to stay in the upper levels of the class, at least it hadn't been a mistake that she had been admitted.

She had also begun to spend time with another student, Greg, a handsome young man whom many of the girls admired. He seemed interested in her, and they gradually spent much of the little free time there was together. He made some sexual overtures to her, but she couldn't decide what to do. She felt attracted to him, but had really felt she wanted to remain a virgin. She talked with her roommate who supported this position. One night some friends said they had seen Greg with another girl. Janet was hurt and she confronted him. He said he had never meant their relationship to be exclusive. She felt shocked and shaken—the sexual invitation had meant to her that they were really "serious." She was relieved she had said "no." Later that year she began to see Tom, a fellow student on the same corridor. At first it was a studying together relationship. Tom, however, wanted more of her time. She felt competitive and anxious at his easy academic success, flattered and also a bit constrained at his interest and demands. They spent a weekend alone in his family's house which led to sexual intimacy but not intercourse. Janet still had reservations about sex but felt much more comfortable thinking of it with Tom, who seemed to give and wish more, and clearly felt some commitment.

Over the summer she met Alex and was surprised at how strongly she felt about him and he about her. She felt it was much more "grown up" and thought her feelings before had been based on dependency and "puppy love." The sexual relationship which they developed seemed "natural" and not in violation of her earlier feelings. The balance of dependency and freedom and toler- ance of each other's need for privacy as well as sustained interest or caring was new for her in a relationship. Alex, for his part, had had several brief relationships that involved some sexual intimacy and, in two instances, led to sexual intercourse. He felt no particular emotional attachment, however, until he met Janet, and had even wondered whether he was capable of "love." With Janet he recognized feelings of affection and admiration that went well beyond simple sexual interest, but he was still not convinced that his feelings represented a permanent commitment.

Janet and Alex maintained an exclusive relationship through- out the sophomore year, and discussed living together during junior year but decided not to, partly because Janet was concerned about her parents' reaction and did not want to dissemble. Alex felt that this was ridiculous but he accepted Janet's decision. They continued to see each other during the junior year, but the frequency and intensity seemed to decrease. Toward the end of this period, they agreed to date other people if the opportunity seemed right. During the summer Janet became romantically involved with a slightly older man who was a junior executive in the place where she worked. This seemed like a more mature relationship to her and for the first time she seriously considered the possibility of marriage. Alex, when he learned about Janet's new relationship, felt quite resentful, and responded by dating as many different women as he could, partly with the hope that Janet would see him and feel jealous.

When at Christmas Janet confided to Alex that she was engaged, he became very hurt and depressed. Gradually, however, he came to realize that he was really not ready for marriage and with this realization his feelings about Janet changed. He recognized that the relationship with her had freed him emotionally, and as a result much of his anger and jealously disappeared. He and Janet were able to reestablish a friendship and each acknowledged to the other how important their relationship had been in the maturing process.

Although the above brief vignette is not in any way remarkable, it illustrates some of the developmental issues that are involved in relationships and maturation in the college period. Janet most clearly goes through a process of development in which issues of self-esteem, commitment, sexual experimentation, the capacity for intimacy, and intellectual achievement all play a part. Alex goes through a similar process, but seems only partially to resolve some of these issues. The vignette, however, is incomplete on two counts: it gives no information about early development which has great influence on the form that relationships in college will take, and it says nothing about the post-college outcome of these experiences. Although it is implied that Janet is ready for commitment and Alex is not, time might show that Janet's commitment was the premature one and Alex's response more adaptive in the longer view. The following consideration of adolescent development will attempt to provide a framework for an understanding of relationships in college.

First, some theoretical concepts are needed. Development can be conceptualized as a process which continues throughout life with certain critical issues characteristic of each phase of the cycle. Ideally, the developmental tasks of one phase are resolved, and are succeeded by a new set of challenges. In practice, however, the resolution is never complete and the residue of unresolved issues from one stage influences the ways in which the person copes with the next. No attempt will be made to describe fully the early stages of development, but the issues that are especially important for understanding late adolescence and early adulthood will be outlined.

There are a number of theoretical models for understanding personality development. Some of these models are behavioral, focusing on observed changes in behavior; some, such as that of Kohlberg and Gilligan,[5] trace moral development, and others, such as that of Perry,[6] trace intellectual and psychological development. Psychoanalytic views of psychosexual development by Freud,[7] Erikson,[8] Anna Freud,[9] Blos,[10] Mahler et al.,[11] and others postulate unconscious dynamic forces as essential to understand maturation and attempt to integrate psychological drives, biological factors, genetic endowment, personal experience and societal influences. The recent contributions of Kohut[12] place particular emphasis on the lifelong role of early relationships in development and, specifically, their influence in determining a person's sense of self-worth.

Failure to cope with important developmental tasks in adolescence has significant consequences in adult life, but people pass through developmental stages at different rates so that not all college students will have reached the same developmental points at the same time. In clinical work, one tries to favor growth in a direction that is judged broadly appropriate, but the manner in which psychological issues are resolved varies considerably from person to person. The best possible resolution for a given individual will not necessarily conform to a postulated theoretical "norm." Rigid adherence to theories that propose universally applicable stages and timetables of development has been criticized as overlooking the variations introduced by culture, social class, history, and individual differences. Nevertheless, in tracing development, it is conceptually helpful to consider that certain age or stage appropriate tasks dominate a particular period.

In the transition to adulthood, the adolescent must become established as a separate, integrated individual, with the capacity to form meaningful relationships, and also to be alone, and to function autonomously. This balance of autonomy and relatedness is extremely important, and is a theme that will recur frequently in the discussion of various relationships. In order to understand this process one must turn to the individual's early development and trace the implications of earlier phases for later adaptation. Blos has written that the chief developmental task of adolescence is "the second individuation process."[13] He compares it to the first individuation phase, described by Mahler as occurring around ages one to two at which time one attains a sense of self and a sense of the constancy of those around one.[14] Blos, in a more recent paper, speaks of the greater potential for identification of the girl compared with the boy. In the typical course of women's development "relatedness" has remained more prominent in the balance of autonomy vs. relatedness than it does for men.[15]

## Early relationships

The first important relationship to a developing human being is the mother*-infant relationship. However, almost from birth onward, if the infant is to develop psychologically into a self-sustaining individual, it is necessary for the infant to begin to separate from the mother. In addition to the mother's role, the active participation of a father or any other care-taking person, such as an older sibling, can also play an important part in furthering the young child's accomplishing the tasks of development.

   Initially, the infant is psychologically and physically in a close reciprocal relationship with the other in which each is responsive to the other, until the child begins to be able to move about. Even very young infants can recognize their caretakers and respond differentially. When emerging motor development and maturation make crawling and walking possible, the toddler begins to

---

*The word "mother" is used throughout this discussion to refer to the most important caretaker who does not have to be the biological mother.

practice leaving and returning to the mother, and is able to tolerate physical distance from her with the assurance that she is still available. Once this relationship is established, the toddler can then separate from the mother in the psychological sense, which is called individuation.[16]* The child gradually becomes able to conceptualize himself or herself internally as an autonomous human being, i.e., as a person who is separate from mother and able to provide some of his or her own gratifications. This first sense of individuation, while it is initially established by eighteen months of life, is further consolidated over the next two years or so. Moreover, these important issues are thoroughly reworked in adolescence and, indeed, may be reworked throughout the life cycle.

Before true separation and individuation can occur, the child must develop a sense of the predictability and constancy of important people in the environment. Erikson, addressing the events of the same period, describes the need to develop "basic trust" before moving on to the next phase which he characterizes as involving struggles for autonomy and the conflicts generated by independence, eventually progressing to "taking initiative."[17] The child, after achieving relative mastery of the process of a two-person relationship, usually moves on through the so-called oedipal stage which involves forming differential relationships with mother and father. The child, then, becomes part of a triangular configuration, rather than relating to each parent in a one-to-one fashion only. It is in this phase that the relationship with the parent of the opposite sex becomes eroticized, and the one with the parent of the same sex becomes competitive.

A brief digression is in order to clarify the psychoanalytic concept of childhood sexuality. Childhood sexuality does not

---

*In the literature various terms are used without clear agreement on definition. Separation is used here in the sense of physical, external separation. Individuation refers to psychological separateness.

mean a genital sexual relationship. Rather, a broader meaning is intended, one that refers to a whole range of activities, feelings, and fantasies beginning in infancy and continuing into adult life. At each phase of development it takes different forms. The infant has a capacity for a variety of bodily pleasures, principally organized around being taken care of, being fed, and establishing a primary bond to a mothering person. Bodily stimulation, being held, cuddled, and the pleasure of warm skin contact are experienced, and the feelings thus engendered remain as components of adult sexual pleasure in later life. Early childhood sexual experiences are not orgastic in the adult sense. They are, however, referred to as sexual because they contain precursors of orgastic pleasure and because they contain components of adult sexual responses, such as kissing and caressing. In the oedipal phase of development, the child's relationships to parents are organized around interim and complex feelings of love, rivalry and admiration. These feelings can either be conscious and expressed directly or unconscious and expressed via dreams or in fantasy via stories and fairy tales.

As development proceeds, the child gradually gives up, in part, the more unrealistic aspect of wishes for intimacy and physical possession of the parent of the opposite sex. At the same time, the relationship with the parent of the same sex may become less of a rivalry and more of a friendly attachment with identification with that parent. This may form the prototype for later friendships with members of the same sex to some extent. Siblings have important concomitants in relationships. Many of the family configurations play an important role in later life, such as whether a person is first born or last born influences self-concept as the oldest and most competent, or the "baby" to be indulged. Some of these are later reproduced in friendships. Freud believed that it was out of the resolution of this stage of development, and the triangles which are part of it, that the child emerged with a definite sense of gender identity of which one important component was the identification with the parents and internalization of their values.[18] More recent research, however, has shown that gender identity itself is typically established earlier in life and is usually irreversible by eighteen to twenty-four months of age.[19] The child continues to learn the ramifications of gender identity throughout childhood.

By the end of the oedipal period, the child loves, or at least is capable of loving, not only the parents but also other children of the opposite sex.

Erikson divides the life cycle into a series of stages, each characterized by crises or turning points which have two possible resolutions paired as antagonists, such as basic trust vs. mistrust, and autonomy vs. shame and doubt.[20] He focuses on the developmental task of adolescence as the problem of integrating the roles and skills learned in the earlier stages with those of the adult world. The two outcomes of this stage at the end of adolescence are "ego identity vs. identity diffusion" and he describes it as a process of integrating childhood identifications, basic drives, pubertal changes, and the demands of the adult social world. The process includes the establishment of a solid gender identity— that is, a sense of masculinity or femininity—and an occupational identity.[21]

## Adolescence

Adolescence is ushered in by the biological changes of puberty when, under the impact of hormonal changes, the individual experiences a growth spurt toward adult shape and size and develops the secondary sex characteristics of the adult man or woman.[22] Hair and fat distribution change, genitals increase in size, menstruation begins in girls, and seminal emissions in boys. These biological changes are accompanied by overt sexual fantasies and feelings, by increased sexual tension, and by a number of psychological changes.

Blos notes that the physical fact of puberty evokes anxiety, which causes the adolescent to undergo a psychological regression.[23] As part of this process, earlier relationships with parents are idealized. However, in the interest of individuation, the negative aspects of the relationship with parents become emphasized and the positive aspects may be projected onto extrafamilial figures. Sometimes this projection of an idealized or romanticized view of an earlier relationship with the parent takes the form of an adolescent crush or leads to the idealization of an older person as a preferred parent surrogate. Eventually, reality will simply not sustain the idealized views. The adolescent, therefore, begins to disengage psychologically from the external and internalized ties to earlier important figures (usually parents) and to embark on finding new and extrafamilial people to love and relate to in the outside world.

This second individuation process is accompanied by an acceleration of maturation with the appearance of new emotional and adaptive capacities and major cognitive growth. This maturation, in turn, makes it less desirable or necessary to return to the now outmoded and partially abandoned gratifications of childhood. New relationships become especially important, and these, in turn, promote further maturation. As the adolescent turns away from depending on earlier idealizations of self and important other people, he or she may search for an answer to the unspoken question, "What do I want to be like?"

Peers are very important during school years and provide a crucial source of learning about gender role, social mores, and skills, Throughout adolescence the peer group continues to be critically important. Blos has said, "The peer group is the substitute, often literally, of the adolescent family."[24] In the peer group the adolescent practices new roles and forms of identification without the necessity for permanent commitment to any one role. Childhood relationship patterns, in which there is a high degree of unbalanced dependency and less well-defined separateness from parents, are abandoned, althogh unevenly. Many college experiences contribute to this process. Experiences which accentuate one's differences from others reinforce the still uncertain sense of self as a separate person.

It is important to realize that individuation does not mean isolation. It is an internal process and leads to the potential for a kind of autonomous relatedness, in which people come together as individuals for meeting mutual needs and sharing interests. Isolation usually results from difficulty in forming relationships and an inability to achieve this important balance of autonomy and relatedness.

Thus, a person who lives physically alone may actually be closely tied to others and unable to make independent decisions. Conversely, students who live at home and interact daily with their families may nevertheless differentiate themselves from parental patterns and separate from family ties psychologically as effectively as the student in a dormitory setting. Peer relationships—friendships, romantic involvements, and casual interchange with others in the environment—have a crucial role in this process.

A further aspect of the establishment of autonomy is the process in which the individual's own psychological boundaries become more clearly established and strengthened. This, in turn, enhances the capacity to form close, intimate relationships since the threat of losing oneself in a relationship is lessened. The ability to relate as a separate person with a firm sense of self is only gradually achieved and adolescent relationships themselves form the crucial context in which it occurs. The ties to the family are not ruptured, but are redefined.

In addition to individuation, there are other developmental tasks of late adolescence. All tend to be interrelated and to dovetail one into the next. Individuals develop with different facets of personality dynamically balanced, and it distorts the integrated ways in which human personality is organized to separate these tasks into discrete categories. However, for purposes of discussion, they will be considered separately under the following headings:

- cognitive development
- development of self-esteem
- consolidation of gender identity and sexual orientation
- the capacity for intimacy
- capacity for commitment
- achievement of a consistent personality organization

## Cognitive development

Students go to college to learn, and educators hope that the college experience will not only add to their knowledge, but also will inculcate an ability to think complexly and gain new appreciation of ideas. At first glance, cognitive development and the development of relationships seem to have little in common, except that they may occur simultaneously in the same individual. Closer scrutiny, however, reveals that they tend to be intimately linked.

The enormously increased cognitive development allows the adolescent more readily than the child to try out in fantasy various roles and to engage in more realistic self-observation. Perry in his studies of college students has focused on the intertwining of intellectual and psychological development.[25] He observes that younger students, particularly freshmen, tend to employ dualistic modes of thinking. They look rather dogmatically for the one and only Truth and tend to reject alternative views as false, if not morally reprehensible. Perry observes during the second individuation process of adolescence a similar "splitting" of ideas and values into all-good and all-bad, as that characterized by Mahler as occurring in early childhood.[26]

As students proceed in college, Perry observes that they enter an intermediate phase of development, becoming disillusioned with the inadequancies of their absolute approach to Truth. They then begin to think that all views are relative, and that one opinion, interpretation, or scientific theory is as good as another.[27] In a later phase of development, they gradually begin to comprehend that some evidence, some methods, and some investigations have been arrived at more carefully than others and, therefore, these serve as a better basis for predictions or furnish better explanations about natural and social events. Thus, students achieve the ability to evaluate theories or ideas, and assign greater value to complex, rather than simple, modes of thinking. This ability leads ideally to the capacity for commitment to a particular set of values for oneself.

The intellectual activity of college evokes emotional as well as cognitive responses. Freshmen often approach even abstract theoretical ideas very much from the perspective of the *feelings* these ideas arouse in them. Assertions that run counter to what they *wish* to hold true may be hotly debated, slighted, or distorted. For example:

> A law professor sought help from a colleague in his efforts to convey both sides of a complex problem of uncertainty about laws protecting reproductive capacity in work situations. When he raised questions with the class about future effects of hazards which might not be known at the time when decisions were made, and the more general problems of the kind of information one needed, the students became upset. They wanted one answer to be the right answer, a solution which would protect everyone and which would be based on evidence available immediately. "They can't stand it if it can't be the way they want it and the way they feel is right," the professor complained.

Learning through reading may provide ways to search for one's "selfhood." In addition to assigned readings, students often select books about the self, self-expression, and self-development. The spirit of inquiry, curiosity, and the intellectual activities that are central to the educational goals of college can be valued parts of one's personality. They may help a student to find common interests within a relationship and to facilitate communication between individuals, thereby enriching friendship. Intellectual achievement frequently leads to recognition and high class ranking and contributes to the student's positive self-assessment. As does ability in sports or popularity with the opposite sex, academic standing can also lead to enhanced social standing.

To an extent, it appears that the progression of relationships parallels students' cognitive development. In the first phase, authorities, teachers, parents, and other "role model" adults may be seen in starkly contrasting colors. They may be accepted relatively unconditionally as heroes or as "right" or rejected as having nothing to contribute if not downright "wrong" or even "evil." This orientation is consistent with viewing those peers who belong to the "in-group" as worthy of trust and allegiance and considering others as people to be avoided if not as objects of actual hostility. An example:

> A housing unit formed around the concept of foreign language use had been established by an admired faculty member. It was threatened with dissolution, presumably because of residents' apathy. This aroused the freshmen in the group to loud protests and complaints that the faculty resident advisor was to blame. The previously placid house became a beehive of activity as the students turned against the resident fellow and sought out a new, involved committed resident assistant who helped formulate a new program and helped "save" the house. In the process, the previously revered faculty resident as well as the dean of housing became objects of scorn as they were accused of not letting the students know what was expected of them. This represented a sharp change of attitude and shifting of blame.

The second, or relativistic, phase brings into play a questioning of these sharp demarcations. Some individuals from the "out-group" can become objects of interest, or, possibly, of friendship. In more extreme cases, an almost indiscriminate experimenting with all sorts of relationships may occur. In the third phase, there is a movement toward stronger relationships, usually with fewer people. Above all, there is at least the beginning of a commitment to one or a few persons for deeper, more sustained, more mutually open relationships, and potentially to a direction in one's life. This does not imply that to be "normal" all students must form a commitment to someone by the end of college, but it envisions an increased capacity for such commitment. Obviously, the attainment of Perry's last phase of cognitive development presumes a relatively clear-cut sense of individuation and self, which helps such relationships to develop.

## The development of self-esteem

Self-esteem is the feeling and attitude one has about oneself and is believed to result from the degree of correspondence between how one sees oneself and one's concept of the "ideal self" or how one would like to be. The individuation process involves the achievement of a relatively clear-cut sense of self, including some ideas about how this self is regarded by others. If the sense of self approximates the ideal or wished-for self, then individuals feel good about themselves, and self-esteem is high. If the opposite is true, then self-esteem is low. Self-esteem derives from a number of sources and varies during different periods of life. During adolescence, self-esteem is particularly changeable and vulnerable. In part, this is because one's self-concept and ego ideal fluctuates as one shifts away from parental views in the process of exploring and establishing one's own set of values. In part, it is also particularly responsive to the views others have about oneself before a solid sense of one's own "identity" is consolidated.

The concept of the ideal self is derived from relationships with other people. At a young age, children watch the older people they know and care about, and they begin to assimilate ideas on how a "good" person ought to be and ought not to be. The people (usually parents) closest to the child are the models for these first ideas, which are then modified as the child grows and is exposed to other people who can also serve as models.

The resultant internalized complex of images is called the ego-ideal. Self-esteem depends not only on how closely someone matches the ego-ideal but also how well one can learn to tolerate failures to live up to it. Additionally, it will depend on how successfully someone is able to modify the internal ideal itself and, if necessary, to adapt it to new situations. The ego-ideal in adolescence may shift as rapidly as the sense of self. Every new experimental relationship may entail some perception of the other person as someone who is supposedly masterful, good, beautiful, or smart or who embodies some other important aspect of the ego-ideal. The fact that the other person approaches the ego-ideal helps the student to incorporate some of these qualities and to increase self-esteem through a kind of reflected acceptance by the idealized person.

The achievement of mastery in one or another sphere also contributes to self-esteem. It is obvious that people take pleasure in doing something well if it is important to them. There is pleasure in the accomplishment for itself alone, and a sense of gratification from having been able to do it. Thus, a child learning to walk enjoys both the greater mobility attained, but also feels very good about himself or herself as a being that walks as opposed to one that only crawls. A similar pattern is evident in intellectual, emotional, and interpersonal achievement at older ages. One can both enjoy a new relationship and feel pleasure in having been able to form it.

In college there are many arenas—academic, extracurricular, and social—in which there are opportunities for mastery. Some, such as academic and athletic, provide certain objective measures, for example, grades or varsity sport status. Others, such as social, may be less measurable, but even in this sphere, election to clubs or fraternities may confer a public mark of "success." Each person sets specific goals and standards, and meeting (or exceeding) them is a source of pride and pleasure and promotes a sense of well-being. Matching others' expectations and being judged well by others confirms the feeling of self-worth. Obviously, the opposite is also true. The expectations of others can thus serve a positive or a negative function. Students who have low expectations of themselves and of whom not enough is expected by others may not be sufficiently motivated to realize their capacities fully. Students who feel too much is expected of them may always feel some sense of failure despite evidence of considerable external success. By the time college is reached, each individual has had many experiences tending to produce or to undermine a positive self-image, and they will vary widely in the resulting feelings of self-esteem.

After considerable vicissitudes, the shifting ego-ideal and sense of self will eventually stabilize. Under these circumstances, self-esteem will become more stable and firmly established, although fluctuations in self-esteem continue throughout life, rising and falling in relation to external success and failure, or sometimes independent of objective events but in reaction to the lifelong internal process of measuring oneself against one's ego-ideal. The internal process is never the only determinant. People always remain somewhat responsive to others' regard of them, but in adolescence outside opinions are especially powerful; as the transition to adulthood is achieved, most individuals become less vulnerable to the opinions of others, in part because their sense of self has consolidated.

## Consolidation of gender identity and sexual orientation

An important part of adolescent development is the consolidation of one's gender identity as male or female, and the establishment of a satisfactory sexual orientation.

It is important here to define terms. Sexual identity refers to a person's sense of being male or female, which in turn depends on his or her biological sexual characteristics. In normal development, these form a cohesive pattern so that a person has no doubt about his or her sex. Gender identity, according to Stoller, denotes "psychological aspects of behavior related to masculinity and femininity." Gender identity is social, whereas sexual identity is biological. Stoller states, "most often the two are relatively congruent. That is, males tend to be manly and females, womanly."[28] Gender role behavior is related to and, in part, derived from gender identity and refers to all those actions and feelings in relation to oneself or others which have to do with one's behaving, acting or thinking as a man or as a woman. Thus, it is the gender identity and/or the gender role behavior which undergoes further consolidation in adolescence.

With the onset of puberty and the consequent development of secondary sexual characteristics, bodily changes must be integrated with the existing self-concept and the knowledge of adult gender roles derived from earlier developmental phases. By the time an individual reaches adolescence, he or she has absorbed the culturally determined definition of gender roles through cognitive information and via identifications with important people and many experiences with peers. Gender roles are constantly changing and vary with each culture, and they may change radically within a person's lifetime. Although what are considered acceptable masculine or feminine behavior changes externally—for example, the shift for women from more passive to active styles—individuals usually have internalized residues of previous gender role stereotypes which may create conflict between the changing expectations of the contemporary culture and earlier identifications.

In addition to social influences that shape gender role behavior, there is an internal need to establish within oneself a consistent, acceptable gender identification and a preferred sexual orientation. Although gender identity usually determines the preferred sexual partner, which is usually someone of the opposite sex, some awareness of conflicting, e.g., bisexual, impulses is not unusual during adolescence. To establish the dominance of a particular gender identity one must integrate the components of sexuality that derive from childhood sexuality and from early experiences with both parents. Although it is not yet entirely clear what determines the presence of bisexual impulses, it seems likely that early developmental experiences and identifications influence sexual orientation, which may also be influenced by biological factors. In the usual developmental sequence there is an establishment of a hierarchy of behavior and preference for either a heterosexual or homosexual orientation, which for most individuals is believed to be established before puberty. This implies an inhibition of the potential for other forms of sexual orientation, although in "normal" adolescence there may be some experimentation with the other orientation in fantasy or reality. There is a biological bias toward an adult heterosexual orientation in all nonhuman mammals, and this probably also exists in humans, although it may be more subject to modification by environmental influences.

As the individual reaches the stage of adult sexuality, sexual experiences offer direct rewards in pleasure and also influence the resolution of important developmental issues. Earlier life themes, such as nurturing, acceptance, stimulation, assertion, dominance, submission, and receptivity are enacted in the sexual play of adults. These may also become connected with the capacity for orgasm. All one's life there is a reworking and expression of elements of identity in sexuality.

The experimentation with new gender role behavior, if it is to be maturational, assumes that the developmental tasks described earlier will have helped the individual achieve a firmer sense of self, and the ability to consider gender role choices, as well as the ability to make commitments to these choices. One must have a clear sense that one is a person and an individual in one's own right before one can comfortably express the needs engendered by being a man or a woman, although these are in part simultaneous developments.

## The capacity for intimacy

Intimacy may be described as a subjective state of closeness in which sufficient safety is experienced with another person to allow relaxation of self-boundaries. It is considered an important component of mature relationships and a source of enrichment and nurturance for the individual. To be intimate is to attain gratification of a wish for warmth and relatedness and to have the opportunity for constructive expression of sexual and aggressive drives. Intimacy can exist without sex and certainly sex can exist without intimacy, but the two in combination are usually considered synergistic in their contribution to pleasure and fulfillment in an erotic relationship. Friendships, e.g., nonerotic relationships, can also involve intimacy, even though the concept is more often applied to relationships that have a clear erotic component.

Certain conditions must prevail for the attainment of intimacy. A solid sense of self and the capacity to maintain a self-representation are required. Trust is necessary and the conviction that one will not be painfully intruded upon or destroyed, and also that one need not fear one's own aggression. One must be able to relinquish control temporarily, to allow dependency on another, and to see the other person more or less realistically. One must not be distracted by neurotic misperceptions which can lead to defensive interaction. This, in itself, suggests sufficient maturity to assess another person's needs as well as one's own. Sometimes, intimacy is felt to be dangerous. Without a firm sense of self, a close relationship may be experienced as an actual merging with the other person or as a blurring of boundaries which is too threatening to one's self-definition.

Intimacy is not a fixed or constant state. It partakes of feelings of closeness in the present, some of which are associated with early gratifying experiences of being loved and understood. It usually is attained when one feels sufficiently "free" in oneself while with someone else so that barriers are lowered and one can be open with feelings. In this sense, the experience of intimacy reflects a struggle characteristic of adolescence, that is, between the wish to keep old attachments unchanged, i.e., for the old ties to remain, and at the same time the wish for change, for separateness, and for developing one's own identity, all of which are enhanced by relationships with new people.

While it is difficult if not impossible to "measure" whether or not an individual has achieved intimacy because it is a subjective state, the capacity to achieve intimacy denotes a high level of personality development which profoundly affects the quality of the person's relationships throughout the rest of life. Although intimacy occurs within a relationship, both partners do not necessarily share the experience equally. One partner may describe a relationship as intimate, while the other may not. This may result from a need to feel intimate, from a greater capacity for intimacy, or simply from misperception.

A common element in intimate experiences is the sense of closeness in which differences can be acknowledged but are temporarily ignored in the service of a goal, which is, in broad terms, to be able to love actively or to be loved as one imagined one was as an infant, only in the present and better. Attempts to develop intimacy probably always raise questions as to whether one is lovable. Relationships which confirm one's feeling of lovability enhance self-esteem.

Where a sexual relationship forms the context of the intimate experience, the same meanings still pertain. This situation, however, is unique because of the mutually agreed upon goal of specific drive release and satisfaction. Physical contact can serve to enrich the memories of being held and loved and simultaneously challenge the individual to maintain self-boundaries in the context of actual body contact and invasion. A tentative equilibrium is established within each encounter—which may be additionally influenced by other motivations such as achievement, competition, dependency, or the need for experimentation.

## The capacity for commitment

Late adolescence and early adulthood are the life phases in which most people, after a certain amount of experimentation, develop the capacity for commitment—both to a choice of work or career and to a particular relationship. Commitment involves not only positive choice, which may not be easy, but also the ability to close off a host of other possibilities, which may be the more difficult aspect of the task. When, because of incomplete development or revival of early problems, the latter totally fails to occur, the individual may exist in a kind of diffuse state, ricocheting among a variety of possible occupations and a series of relationships. No one of these can meet the requirement of encompassing all possibilities and, therefore, each is unsatisfactory. The success of the commitment to an occupational choice and to a particular role for oneself in interpersonal relationships depends in part on the degree of individuation that has been attained. This means having a relatively clear-cut sense of who one is and who one wants to be, and usually is achieved only after trying out, first in fantasy and perhaps later in action, various styles. Sometimes commitment occurs in the service of individuating from parents, and the choice is determined by the need to have parents disapprove. This often is "pseudo-commitment" which is given up once the individual feels secure in the individuation process.

Perhaps most importantly, commitment means that the individual has achieved the ability to give up a sense of omnipotence wherein, at least in fantasy, all roles are possible, and one is all things to all people. If a commitment is made when one has achieved a relatively stable sense of identity as well as the ability to sort out in a relatively mature and realistic way the most desirable alternatives, then the commitment will have a further maturational effect. If the choice is made on the basis of earlier and more primitive views of oneself and on polarized absolutist views of the world, then the choices are likely to be expressions of earlier repetitive ways of thinking and feeling. Under these circumstances the process of commitment will either not occur, will be fraught with dissatisfaction if it does occur, or may lead to the appearance of symptoms as an expression of internal conflicts.

## Achievement of consistent organization of the personality

The achievement of a consistent personality organization is also a result of the process of maturation and consists of the integration of past self-images in a new way leading, in Erikson's terms, to a consolidation of identity. An organized personality is one in which the disparate elements that contribute to the person's sense of self are more smoothly integrated and consistent, with a more clearly defined personal value system and the ability to recognize one's intentions and motivations as belonging to oneself. This involves a corresponding ability to have a clear sense of one's own priorities, preferences, tastes, and styles, along with the capacity to work, all of which combine to form a particular and unique human being.

Although each phase of development requires that certain conflicts be at least partially resolved if the next phase is to be entered into successfully, the individual must simultaneously retain a dynamic relationship with aspects of self as it existed in earlier phases. Thus, even though someone may appear to break radically with the past in terms of external beliefs, statements of values, or in behavior, it is important that internal alienation from one's earlier psychological self does not result. If the latter occurs, there is the very real danger of a psychological breakdown that may lead to the development of psychiatric illness. Consequently, one of the tasks of this age period is the integration of prior elements of identity. While this occurs to some extent in every age phase, it can be especially difficult in late adolescence when the individual, as his or her world expands, is most intensely bombarded with different values, views, and examples of the behavior of others. Higher education with its built-in base of questioning and inherent skepticism of established thinking may cause special difficulties for a particularly vulnerable individual. The college, however, also creates a context in which support for the process of change may be found in shared experiences with many others undergoing the same process.

Gender differences in individuation and autonomy are part of the classical sex role stereotyping, based on the male model, in which women have both been and are considered less "autonomous," independent, and differentiated as individuals separate from family relationships. Regarding these latter traits as negative may merely reflect the male socialization bias which affects women negatively. Truly important values may be expressed by stressing the importance of connectedness and involvement in relationships; i.e., qualities with which women appear to be especially endowed.

As one develops a sense of identity, becomes aware of one's desires, needs and goals, and achieves a heightened sense of independence, one increasingly must call on one's own resources to achieve these goals and gratifications. This requires developing an effective means of self-assertion and expression of aggression as well as developing ways of coping with aggression in others. One must also be able to modulate one's own aggressive impulses so that they facilitate attainment of aims rather than creating obstacles. Too much aggression can be frightening or self-defeating. If, however, one fails to develop satisfactory self-assertion, one runs the risk of fulfilling few needs and of becoming increasingly discouraged, or of needs being fulfilled sporadically as a result of external events, thereby decreasing one's sense of control and mastery and increasing the feeling of being largely at the mercy of whims of chance. The inner sense of being in control of oneself and one's life is important in reinforcing self-confidence, which in turn clarifies one's identity.

Developing effective self-assertive mechanisms has been a

particularly complex problem for women, who have been more conflicted in the expression of aggression, and have had difficulty in acknowledging and directly expressing their own needs. Although this has been changing and most students no longer consider it unfeminine to be aggressive in certain ways, inner conflicts remain. For most women, recognition of their aggression creates a sense of guilt and diminished self-esteem.

Moral issues must also be considered. For example, decisions about sexual behavior vastly influence one's self-esteem as measured in terms of moral worth. These assessments are in turn a reflection of the individual's moral development. Ideally, all these components of experience will integrate relatively harmoniously.

## Summary

In this somewhat idealized overview of important areas of adolescent development, the focus has been on some of the major developmental tasks. It is important to emphasize that the main issue of late adolescence is to develop the capacity to live as a full person outside one's original family and to establish oneself in society. This process is not necessarily smooth; each phase of development has the potential for regression, and the consequent reworking of that which has preceded it. In coping with the anxiety which is aroused in the course of development, the person makes use of a variety of defenses, which may be transient, or may be incorporated as a permanent part of the personality. One must also recognize that the kind of development involved will be a reflection of the kind of adult a particular society wants. In a society such as ours, where differentiation and independence are valued, these values strongly affect the developmental process of adolescence.

It is critical that all who work with college students—whether psychiatrists, counselors, teachers, institutional administrators, or other students—be aware that the new opportunities for trying out roles may result in further maturation, in temporary regression in the service of maturation, or in the regressive repetition of earlier forms of relationships. Infrequently, it may result in symptom formation, such as depression, insomnia, lack of concentration, and a variety of other emotional difficulties. It is hoped that this report may point out some ways in which the college experience may maximize the possibility that new relationships will lead to further maturation.

# 3

## THE TRANSITION FROM HOME TO COLLEGE

Students say that among their chief reasons for going to college is the exposure to different ideas and to people different from themselves. Through new interpersonal relationships in college, students wish to both widen their own psychological capacities, i.e., to become different themselves, and to enlarge their capacity for empathy and intercourse with others. Relationships during this period reflect both a sense of who one is as well as who one is seeking to become. In some ways the security of home continues to be sought, while in other ways the goal is separation from the family for the sake of establishing one's own individuality.

### Choice of college and area of study

Even in anticipation a college can either become invested with qualities of parental values or represent new values in the student's search for personal identity. Thus, before the student leaves home the developmental issues may become sharply focused in the process of selecting a school as in the following:

> Bruce, the oldest of three children, chose a school in the South, surprising his New England parents who had expected him to follow the family pattern of staying close to home. He expressed a previously unfocused interest in doing research on medically-related topics. His grandmother, whom he had loved and to

whom he had been very close, had died the previous year of an incurable illness. In wanting to try a new part of the country he was expressing the wish for exploration, independence, and literally separating from the family and the family tradition. At the same time he was focusing his interests in a direction which indicated his strong involvement with a family member who had gone.

Family reaction to choice of college may also cause some unexpected reactions from the college-bound student:

Mary Lou had grown up in an environment where it was not customary to go away from home to college. Her family had prospered professionally and her mother's upwardly striving aspirations led her to suggest to her daughter that she look into the best schools away from home. May Lou reacted with bewilderment and reacted as though she interpreted her mother's suggestions as an attempt to cast her out from the home or as punishment for past misdeeds.

Many students do not in fact literally leave home. Over the last decades, the number of college students in residential institutions has increased but not as rapidly as the number of college students in community colleges or those who commute to college. Issues of separation-individuation and the importance of resolving these issues, exist for the student who attends college without ever leaving either the home town or parental home as well as the student away from home. Staying at home does not necessarily interfere with the student's becoming a more autonomous person. One commuting college, The City College of New York, has among its graduates a number of leaders in all fields of the arts, sciences, professions and politics. Many of these students were the first generation of their families ever to attend college, and they either lived at home or within a five-mile radius of their family and the college. Yet they were apparently able to attain a degree of psychological separation from parental values which allowed for a high degree of individuation and autonomy.

For many commuting students these developmental tasks were accomplished with great difficulty. Often parents of students from immigrant backgrounds more or less directly objected to and even interfered with the students' "foolish wish" to better themselves. Sometimes the converse was true and students were burdened by such parental pressures to succeed that they could not tell whether college was attended for their sake or the sake of the parents. For commuting students and those in community colleges today similar pressures exist, but currently they are more likely to be felt by the first black child or the first woman in the family to seek a college education rather than a second generation individual from an immigrant background.

The choice of school also may be a reflection of the student's self-concept. External factors, such as finances, intellectual capabilities, or physical liabilities may limit the student's choice of a school. This may result in frustration or loss of self-worth. Clarifying such issues so that the real problems are separated from those of self-esteem promotes a more realistic appraisal for the individual and enhances coping skills.

Identification with parents may be reflected not only in the choices a student makes about colleges but also about fields of study. There may also be a complicated interaction as the following illustrates:

> Alice, the middle of three daughters, was always vague about what she wanted to do. The daughter of two practicing successful artists, she had hesitated between art school and a liberal arts college. She did not feel she could compete with her parents, nor measure up to her academically accomplished sisters. She chose a large university with a diversity of programs which would allow her to explore her own talents. Although her first year there was gratifying, she soon found she became impatient with many of the academic courses. She began to take art classes, in the safety of the new environment, where she would not be compared to anyone. She realized she had genuine talent, and by the end of the second year had decided to transfer to an art school, free to express her identification with her parents, yet having felt this was her own decision as well.

Sometimes the choice of college is influenced by unconscious motives and does not represent a choice which is harmonious with the student's current conscious wishes. In the prior example the wish to avoid competition with her parents motivated her choosing a school which was different from their careers, which she could later change. Growth in the student brings change in interests. Latent conflict with parents may then be displaced onto the subject matter and the student may have difficulty studying effectively until the issues are clarified and separated. All are familiar with the student who is pre-med because of family pressure and consistently flunks chemistry despite a high scientific aptitude.

## College choice in relation to family

The choices the student makes at college of living style, friends, and academic interest may also represent, consciously or otherwise, an emulation of, or rebellion against, parents. Early notions of the "good" or "bad" parent are explored and expressed in the adolescent framework. The student typically modifies his or her prior idealization of parental positions, often going to the opposite extreme of devaluing these positions and the parents as well. The following will illustrate this:

> Susan was the daughter of a successful lawyer from an upper middle-class suburb, having graduated from an exclusive private school emphasizing social contacts as well as academic affairs. She had been preoccupied with dates, appearance, the "right" friends, supported in this by her mother, who also accompanied her on frequent shopping trips, in which she was allowed to have all the latest fashionable clothes. There was considerable tension in the family; Susan never felt as favored as her older or younger brothers. Her mother hid a chronic depression under a well-dressed, polished veneer.
>
> When she chose a college, her "best" choice was a school which supported academic values but also contained many politically

active students. Susan felt lost at first but found herself in sympathy with a group which picked up her latent resentment about the way the women in her family were treated and her parents' upwardly mobile, pressured life style. Although she herself loved the nice clothes and opportunities which came with financial means, she allied herself with more radical groups partly because their values seemed genuinely more appealing and "right," and partly as a clear differentiation from the world of her parents.

For months she argued with her father when she visited home, criticized her mother, and attacked her brothers' career choices. Eventually she began to see that she was not really compatible with the radical groups, and chose a major which led to a clear career path working in a scientific field. By this choice she both accepted certain values consonant with the family but felt sufficiently differentiated.

While excursions into opposite thought and behavior are felt by the student to represent a new maturity, they can in fact be part of the reworking of old issues from childhood as the adolescent moves toward adulthood. Eventually there may be some return of the pendulum to a less extreme position.

Individuation is not only an important psychological process, but also reflects a cultural value of viewing insufficient separation from parents as a developmental failure. Traditionally, this has unquestionably applied to men; however, conventional views of women have not expected the same degree of separation as a part of successful development in contrast to men's. At least for the present, women's psychological needs seem to result in greater affiliation with and dependence on their family. This may reflect women's psychological development, a reaction to cultural constraints, or a combination of these factors. In some cultures individuation usually takes place without the same degree of actual separation expected in American society. The clash of cultural expectations does not always occur when one leaves for college. Sometimes it happens at graduation, as the following example illustrates:

Hanae from an Asian-American background finished four years of
college and wanted to go to graduate school. She reacted with rage
and depression to her parents' insistence that she return home as
soon as possible to give another member of the family a chance to
complete his education. She had assimilated new values from her
college experience, and the idea that she had to submit completely
to her parents and forego personal ambitions for the good of the
family was no longer acceptable. From her parents' standpoint,
however, the fact that she went away to school did not affect her
responsibility to her parents or alter the life plan that they had set
for her.

The process of establishing a separate identity does not occur
all at once. The inner complex ties to family are only gradually
resolved under the impact of new experiences and new development, and college provides a trial period where separation can be
combined with return, where a new place to live can coexist with
the old one, where the "permanent address" representing
permanent ties still remains and differs from the current locus of
life. Even when students live at home, a large part of their time is
spent at school, and relationships with family change.

Freshman year is unique for at least two reasons. It is both the
first year at a new place, and it is the first year away from home,
family, and familiar people and places. Even for those individuals who have been away before, symbolically at least, college
represents the start of the permanent surrender of childhood ties,
which will lead eventually to adulthood. Learning to cope with
the new challenges and people in college is the other side of the
freshman experience. Most of the behavior patterns observed in
freshmen reflect responses to these two predominant issues.
However, different students will be at different points in their
internal personal psychological development while they are in
the same external life phase so that some freshmen have already
accomplished what others have only begun.

The initial separation creates many mixed feelings. Positive
involvement with the new environment, activities, experiences,

and friends may be accompanied by anxiety and excitement and exhilaration in response to expanded horizons and by confusion as values are challenged and loyalties tested. The questioning of what once was accepted and the feeling that one may be rejecting one's past and family by changing and forming new attachments can lead to internal conflict. These inner struggles are sometimes conscious but are quite often unconscious, and they find expression in a variety of individual modes. Sexual values and behavior, attitudes toward drinking and drug use, religious patterns and beliefs, moral and political views can all act as a base for establishing differences from parents. Convictions, stereotypes, and prejudices derived from parental attitudes become unsettled by confrontation with new people and new ideas. New positions taken by the student may reflect not only ambivalence toward family values, but also more objective evaluations of issues as a result of receiving new cognitive information.

## New views of home: fantasy and reality

Adolescents and young adults have difficulty seeing their parents as people. Memories of childhood dependencies and struggles color their view. Their parents' own inner conflicts may be denied, because it is uncomfortable to see the parents as if they were contemporaries with similar anxieties and problems. During the college period the separations and returns home offer the student the oportunity to know parents as individuals, viewed by new criteria, and with some greater distance:

> Barbara was a sad looking, bewildered young woman who came to the Health Center because she could not stop inducing vomiting. She had realized that she had begun to gain weight rapidly soon after her arrival in college so she tried to stop her weight gain by vomiting, but then was unable to stop vomiting. She had been particularly close to her mother who had always

confided in her and hoped that by going to college she would be
spared her mother's unhappy life. Barbara knew full well that
mother was disappointed in father and that she was isolated and
without friends when Barbara left. She pictured mother quite
alone and helpless without Barbara to comfort her. While Barbara
desperately wanted to go to college and get on with her studies,
she felt consciously guilty about leaving her mother to carry on in
her absence, while on another level she clung to the idea that she
was indispensable to her mother. It took a few psychotherapeutic
sessions to clarify Barbara's ambivalence so that she could become
involved in her new life. She called home and discovered, to her
surprise, that mother had resumed some old friendships and apparently was doing quite well, even in Barbara's absence. Barbara
made new friends in the dormitory and discovered that she was
not quite as lonely and homesick as she had been before. The
vomiting stopped.

Fantasies about the parent can be distinguished from the real
parent, sometimes with relief and sometimes with disappointment. Friends, and their reactions, representing the students' current world, become a testing ground for a new assessment of
parents and of the old "family" world. Conversely, friends are
also viewed through the eyes of parents, and this may affect the
student's judgment about the friends chosen:

Martha, who came from the Midwest, invited her father to a
college father-daughter weekend at an Eastern school. She had
idealized him as a powerful, successful and romantic man. She
was reluctant to see that he barely spoke to any of the other fathers
and seemed excessively concerned with the status and prestige of
those he chose to speak to. She noted with distress that he hardly
related to anyone and was uncomfortable with anyone who was
different from himself. When there was a similar event for mothers
and daughters, she saw to her surprise that the depressed,
irrational woman she thought her mother to be, with whom she
had many conflicts at home, was able to participate and be interested in new activities. Her mother was able to relate to new

people and, was really interested in her daughter's college experiences. Martha's idealization of her father was shaken, with consequent depression, but a new relationship with her mother began.

The discontinuities between the world parents grew up in and the world college students now face are all too evident in some of the confrontations between parents and the college environment. Parents may find co-residential living or the campus styles of dress and/or behavior distressing, and the student may be caught in a conflict of loyalties. As was indicated earlier, models which students might find helpful in exploring future roles may be lacking. This is particularly true of women, where life alternatives have changed. Mothers may pressure daughters to achieve in traditional success terms, e.g., marriage and children, or may, at present, because of frustrations in their own lives, have changed their expectations for their daughters and have become the source of pressure for academic success of advancement via careers.

These are real dilemmas for the female student who is trying to sort out old family influences and who may simultaneously be subjected to peer pressure to embark on a career. Vastly greater numbers of women now expect to have careers, but cannot anticipate the conflicts that will be entailed; neither can they resolve the details of the complexity in their lives that will be created until they are in the midst of it. There have been few sources for help with this process, although there is increasing attention to the problems of integrating family and career goals.

## Real changes in the family

In addition to fantasies that the student has about the family, the *actual* events taking place at home are important. Students in college must face real changes in their parents as well as in themselves. Most parents of college students are at midlife with their own midlife experiences, and, possibly crises. Midlife divorce is becoming more frequent. Some parents put off divorce until the children are out of the house, not realizing the impact that this will have on the student involved in the issue of separation from parents. For a student who has left home the breaking up of the family is still potentially very disturbing psychologically, even if it has relatively little impact in practical terms. The student may feel that he or she had some influence in keeping the family together and this may actually be accurate. If so, guilt may result, but, if this is inaccurate, a false sense of omnipotence may follow. A separation disturbs images of parents, and creates realignments. Old childhood competitive feelings or romanticized ties can be revived. If one parent is openly involved in an extramarital relationship, and this is revealed in relation to the divorce, the student may be forced to recognize that parents have active sexual lives, and this, in turn, can be upsetting. Furthermore, the student may feel manipulated by the parents and asked to declare loyalties. For many students, it is important for their family to remain stable while they are exploring separation and independence. The confrontation with problems in the parents' marriage may be particularly difficult at a time when the students are asking themselves how they want to live, whether they want to marry, and what marriage would be like.

Although life expectancy has increased, illness and/or death of parents occur, and these events are inevitably disturbing and disruptive. When students are faced with the challenge of new pursuits and the demands of school, they may feel burdened by parents' real needs and demands which inhibit their freedom, or they may feel guilty or anxious because they are not able to be available and responsive.

One can often see, in the return home for summer or holiday vacations, the student's attempts to practice or try out new ideas and behaviors within the old environment. Sometimes this is met with pleasure and encouragement on the part of the parents, but frequently there are mixed feelings, including strains created by old expectations which are no longer responded to in familiar, once comfortable ways. Visits home can also be used as an emotional "coming back," a time for replenishment and security for the developmentally challenged adolescent who may indulge in a certain regression to earlier more dependent patterns in which he or she was treated as a child by the protective and powerful adults. When these regressions are temporary, they can be comforting and restorative, enabling the student to go back into the world where one must rely on what one carries from home rather than on the actual presence of parents.

The rejection of parental values need not be permanent nor does the turmoil and rebellion of adolescence appear to be universal. Some individuals seem to pass into adulthood without rebellion, and some, with less differentiation from parents. Many later re-embrace parental values out of conscious choice made more freely and thoughtfully than initially. In fact, eventual identification with parents and choices consonant with parental values of occupation, schools, and lifestyle occur very often.

## Initial reactions to college

In anticipating coming to college, the students feel that it is time to find out who they are, and whether they can exist in a rewarding, comfortable sense away from the support of family and friends at home. Every fall, a few freshmen experience an extreme degree of sadness and difficulty in leaving home. These students are bitterly homesick and so focused on missing their families that they cannot think about other things. Paying attention to making new friends or to studying seems unimportant next to their grief. Rarely does this lead to leaving college. Usually, with a little help, these students join their classmates in coping with the feelings which arise on leaving home, and begin to replace their old ties with new ones. Feelings of homesickness, extreme in this small group, are shared to some degree by most students. Although it is adaptive, the eagerness with which freshmen reach out to each other bespeaks the anxiety they all feel as well as their desire for new experience. They are feeling the loss of their child-hood, and even sharing just that with each other is supportive and helpful. To illustrate:

> George came to his Eastern college from a small town in the Mid-west. He was the older of two children, and had had one close friend in school with whom he played chess and shared his ideas and feelings. Otherwise, he had felt shy and out of the mainstream in school, and was dismayed to find that that feeling persisted when he came to college.
>
> His roommate was more outgoing than he, enjoying partying more than studying, so that again George felt "out of it." He was surprised to realize he missed home a lot. At freshman orientation he noticed a quiet, rather pretty woman named Mary, but he was only able to bring himself to speak to her when she reappeared in his English class. They began doing things together, and George was delighted to find they liked each other and had a lot in common. As he felt more comfortable with Mary, he became friends with one of her roommates and began to realize he wasn't thinking about home as much. By Thanksgiving he realized he had made several other friends including Tom, who was in the next room to him and also a chess buff. His friendship with Mary became a sexual relationship, which he enjoyed. He also realized having her as a lover made him feel much better about himself, and helped him overcome much of his initial shyness.

Some freshmen can live without close relationships for a while. They will be slower to jump into relationships just for the sake of the quick security they offer. Others show an urgent need to form a new interpersonal tie as a substitute for the security of home relationships which may even be with a parent-like figure. This fills the void left from leaving home and also acts as a buffer against plunging "naked and alone" into a new and strange environment.

The search for a new source of security may follow various

forms. If the college is residential, meeting one's freshman room-mate (or roommates) is like an arranged marriage. It can be the most anxiety-provoking aspect of the first period. They are going to have to share living space for a whole year, often in one small room in which they have to study, sleep, relax, socialize, and perhaps arrange for the privacy necessary for sexual activity. Sometimes a roommate is the first stranger allowed to share so much of one's life. Students often have exaggerated expectations that a roommate will become a best friend, share many interests, and introduce one to the world of college and sex. Sometimes this happens; more often, at least some of their expectations will not be met. Nevertheless, learning to know and get along with a new person with whom one must share a small space is usually a productive experience—even when it is not a particularly happy one.

Some students come to college and immediately become part of a group. This may be particularly important in a very large college where the size of the student body may feel overwhelming. Identification with the group then may predominate. The members may do most things together, socially and academically. The group provides security and protects the student from both isolation and the anxiety of new encounters. Although the group offers support and emotional interchange, it can be isolating and constricting if too tightly structured, and if loyalty to the group is demanded at the expense of access to other relationships. The group values may be similar to or, as is more likely, strikingly different from parental values. Sometimes the group is quite literally a replacement for former relationships and becomes a kind of substitute family. Feelings and ties to family can some-times be worked out via friends, where the feelings toward friends may be partial displacements from family members. For instance, rivalries with siblings may be expressed in competitive relation-ships with fellow students. A student who has a rejecting and unreachable sibling may attempt to reconstruct a similar relation-ship at school with someone who will be accepting, admiring, and responsive. Other less constructive, competitive patterns also occur, where difficult family constellations are recreated, and frustrating relationships repeated. If it is not possible for the student to change any of these and achieve some mastery of the original family problem, counseling may be indicated.

The confusion, anxiety, and depression which may accompany the transition to college leave students vulnerable to the pseudo-family appeal of cults and religious movements, which promote regression to a less autonomous situation, but provide certainty. The group or peer ideology, even when less encompassing than the sects and cults, can also merely substitute for family values without promoting the student's development of an independent value system. Political movements may also be substitutes for the family by requiring the same dependency and adherence to an externally imposed set of behavior. Ironically, then, the student may consciously appear to be choosing a philosophy or interest which is far removed from the beliefs of his parents, but in actuality the process is recreating the same internal psychological relationship that existed. Therefore, the student remains in the same place developmentally. This is a paradox that may meet the unconscious needs of some students for a more clear-cut, perhaps more rigid or authoritarian family than they actually had. This often seems to occur in instances where the student's own family has been diffuse, disorganized, or unsupportive, and if the family encouraged a kind of premature autonomy that may have been felt as threatening at the time for the student.

When new values, on whatever basis they are held, are different from those of the parents, conflict is likely. If a student enters into relationships which parents find disturbing—such as with individuals of another culture, religion, or race—considerable pressure may be exerted on the student to give up the new alliances which can well alienate the student even further. The student's behavior also may activate memories of the parents' own adolescence which consciously or unconsciously influence their responses.

Some students shift their dependent feelings from home onto one particular friend, and this relationship protects them from fully experiencing the new and unsettling possibilities of the college world. For a few this relationship then may actually hinder development. For others the friendship is less defensive and the support of the friend permits further exploration and discovery.

> Elsie and Polly attended the same in-city private high school. They were very different in their personalities, social outgoingness, even family backgrounds. In high school situations, they were only casual acquaintances. Late in their senior year, after college acceptances and decisions had been made, they recognized they would both be attending the same midwestern college. None of their other friends were heading in the exact same direction. A closeness developed between the two girls based less on shared experiences and interests than anxiety about the future, and the felt need for another person, who was imagined as stronger, to help with the adaptation. The girls asked to room together, and in their first year, were indeed able to provide each other with a sense of family and of things past. They were inseparable. While this arrangement accomplished its support purposes, it inhibited each young woman from her own experimentation and exploration.

> A "little bit of home" had been carried away, which was useful but also deterring to growth. It was not until junior year that Elsie felt secure enough to break away from the comfort of the dyad and try her wings as an individual. This occurred soon after she had entered a fairly stable and gratifying relationship with a young man who seemed to substitute in part for her friend, but also offered a possibility of relating in new ways.

For some, the initial protective relationship may be with a lover. Soon after arrival in college, the student becomes involved in a close, erotic relationship which becomes central. The two are defined as a "couple." They may or may not do everything together, but most of the emotional energy goes into the relationship. These couples frequently do not participate much in group

activities although they may eventually form friendships and
belong to the same circle of friends. Neither may fully wish to
maintain the relationship in its exclusive form, but they are
unable to separate, recognizing to a greater or lesser degree their
mutual dependency. At times, the emotional and sexual
involvement becomes so intense that it precludes effective participation in school work. More frequently they coexist. For some,
the relationship provides security, and the sexual or erotic aspect
is secondary to the dependency. Although to an outsider it may
appear that the students have moved into new relationships and
separated from their families, the relationships also serve to
protect them from a fuller encounter with the new world. The
following is a case in point:

> Meg had come to a large urban university from a small town 100
> miles away. Although a generally good student, she had not
> developed any special areas of competence nor strong interests.
> Her father was a physician and, although warm and affectionate,
> was often unavailable. Her mother was an anxious and dependent
> woman with recurrent depressions. Meg was the older of two
> children, the first to leave home. She had had an ambivalent,
> mutually dependent relationship with her mother.
>
> At first, the university seemed overwhelming. As the blur of
> buildings and people sorted itself out in her eyes, she found she
> shared several classes with Ted. They walked to classes together,
> had lunch together, and soon were dating and then spending
> more of their time together. When Meg brought him home for
> Thanksgiving, her parents were dismayed although they hid their
> feelings at first. Privately they told Meg that Ted didn't seem the
> right sort of boy for her. His family was less well educated, there
> were religious differences, and he did not seem to have clear
> enough goals for his own life.
>
> On return to campus, Meg was in conflict. She felt
> uncomfortable at displeasing her parents, but also angry at their
> criticism. She liked Ted, felt comfortable with him, but most of
> all, did not feel she could stand the loneliness involved in

reentering the huge world of the university alone. After midterms, Meg found she was becoming somewhat bored with the routine of her relationship with Ted, but he pressed her to remain involved with him. She could not resist his dependency either, and so they stayed together until the summer brought a separation and considerable relief to Meg.

Although a few of the early relationships which are formed quickly work out well in the long run, more often they run into difficulties. Because they are formed so precipitously and early, important phases of the development of each individual may well be omitted. These deficiencies in maturation and individuation may have consequences for later life.

Some students may not seem unduly troubled by the loss of home but remain isolated, separate, and continue to feel that they don't "belong." They do not find people with whom they feel they can form relationships. Sometimes, they feel it is not they who cannot adapt, and, instead, project the problem and see the school as cold and disappointing. Such students may concentrate on studying, writing letters home, going for solitary walks, and may define themselves as "loners," or "different." Such a response may be a continuation of an earlier adaptive pattern. If so, they remain in a sense developmentally stuck where they were before coming to college. Although relocated geographically, old patterns and attachments cannot be relinquished, and new ones do not develop. The character of the school environment may influence the outcome of this pattern since some schools are scattered, large and impersonal, while others make more effort to reach isolated students.

Most students are comfortable enough not to need the immediate security of friends so desperately. Usually such students come to college and initially form a variety of more casual, "loose" relationships. This may provide a base for genuine exploration; it may also serve as a protective distance since a social or sexual "whirl" can prevent closer relationships.

However, the student who is able to meet people from different backgrounds, who learns something from most of them, and who becomes friends with some can experience these different environments vicariously. This process furthers the development of the relativism described earlier, in which different values, ideas, and styles are appreciated, and the original, rigid good-bad thinking is replaced. It allows for the development of perspective on one's parents and their values, and furthers the process of independent choice. In short, it represents the appropriate, broadening effect of friendships which one hopes all students will experience eventually, whatever pattern they may use when first entering college.

# 4
# FRIENDSHIP

Having friends is one of the most highly valued attributes of student life. Although not always equally valued by the institution, the capacity for forming friendships is directly related to the other goals of high education, namely the encouragement of growth and expansion. Douvan points out that friendships are distinguished from other kinds of relationships by the absence of universal norms.[29] Thus, it is possible to explore aspects of oneself which are unfamiliar, and to express and affirm these in a variety of new ways. This is more difficult to do in relationships influenced by normative expectations where the rules for behavior are more restricting.

The psychology of friendship has been little studied, and though friendship is often attested to movingly in literature and personal reminiscences, it has rarely been the subject of scientific analysis. *Webster's Third New International Dictionary* defines "friend" as "One that seeks the society or welfare of another whom he holds in affection, respect, or esteem or whose companionship and personality are pleasurable: an intimate associate especially when other than lover or relative" and someone one has known for a time "neither notably intimate nor dependent on business or professional ties."[30] A young woman offered the following improvement on the Webster definition. "A friend is someone who cares about you and about whom you care. It's as simple as that." "Caring" has various degrees of intensity and meaning that may include feelings of warmth,

51

concern, understanding, sharing, need, respect, liking, and loving.

A wide range of relationships is subsumed under the term "friendship" which stands between the most intimate relationship on the one hand and the more casual, less developed relationship usually called acquaintanceship. It is not defined by predetermined blood or contractual tie, but may describe an aspect of an otherwise contractual relationship. A person will sometimes be heard to say "I want to marry someone who is not only a lover but also a friend." On the other hand, English being the confusing language it sometimes is, the addition of boy—or girl—as prefix (e.g., girlfriend, boyfriend) usually connotes an eroticized relationship when it is applied cross-sex. When applied to same-sex relationships, it may be synonymous with the term "friend."

The English language lacks the grammatical form that many European languages possess to distinguish more intimate relationships from the more formal and distant. Thus, in French the use of the "tu" form of address denotes an assumption of closeness, which applies to immediate relatives, lovers, and certain close but noneroticized friendships. English speaking people may not categorize consciously but some kind of unconscious categorization exists based on the character of the relationship because references in ordinary speech will be made to people who are "friends," "close friends," "acquaintances," and "lovers." These words reflect the character of the relationship but do not illuminate its nuances. For example, in a friendship, one person may be clearly dependent on the other, may confide more, and may consider it to be a very special relationship. The less dependent friend may not feel quite the same and may save confidences for another relationship. Furthermore, there are some sex differences in friendship patterns. In this culture, women tend to invest more in relationships; self-sufficiency as an indication of strength is more valued in men than in women; and women are less threatened by intimacy. One suggested explanation for these observations is that aspects of affectionate expression and closeness threaten masculinity by reawakening old feelings of dependency on mother, i.e., a female.

Throughout life, friendships and their functions are also affected by cultural differences. In some groups, a friend is expected to offer much more concrete help than in others. A student from such a group may be disappointed if a fellow student refuses to share possessions or help with academic problems. Family styles can affect the individual's style of relating. Some families value privacy, and personal revelation and openness about feelings or family history is considered generally inappropriate. It is difficult for students from such backgrounds to reveal themselves and to talk about deeper feelings. If a student is anxious about his or her "normality," a not uncommon feeling in adolescence, such self revelation although ultimately reassuring may be particularly painful. Some families pride themselves on their self-sufficiency. Developing a close relationship which seems to involve dependency, therefore, may be perceived as a sign of weakness, and close friendships are seen as risky. Thus, a student coming to college and encountering someone with very different expectations of friendship may be confused, anxious, sometimes pleased, or even overwhelmed at the new possibilities. Changing and expanding one's definition of friendship may contribute significantly to one's sense of autonomy and identity.

## Functions of friendship

In the college years, specific and special functions are fulfilled by friendships, particularly close ones. These are different from those in other life periods. By the end of this period changes should have occurred which render the constancy of an individual's self-esteem and mood to become increasingly independent of external sources. In the process, however, the external sources are highly important. Some want a few really close friends and feel good if they achieve this. For others being generally popular is of great concern, and measures of popularity contribute to these students' self-esteem. These measures may differ for men and women; for example, physical appearance, academic ability, and athletic prowess have been viewed differentially in each sex, and vary from group to group. The individual with a highly valued attribute will inevitably feel some increase in self-esteem, but eventually it would be hoped that self-esteem would become somewhat independent of the immediate group context.

> Arthur has always been an excellent student, but attending elementary and secondary schools in which athletic achievement was almost the only valued attribute, he felt that his intellectual abilities came close to being a handicap. In the small community he lived in, he found almost no one with similar interests and he was frequently ridiculed as a "grind." His only peer relationship was a rather tenuous one in which he tutored a star athlete in algebra. Although he occasionally gained some slight reflected glory from being seen in the star's company, he rightly perceived that the friendship was not solidly based. Thus, high school was a rather miserable experience. Because of his good academic record, he was accepted at a prestigious college, and when he arrived on campus he was astonished to find many students with interests similar to his. Furthermore, his intellectual abilities suddenly became the focus of admiration and respect by his classmates. Although he had always been told that being a good student was important, for the first time he began to experience directly some rewards in the social sphere, which greatly increased his sense of self-esteem.

Friendships play an important role in self-esteem and self-discovery. Self-esteem may also be increased by experiences with groups of friends; belonging to a highly valued group increases an individual's self-evaluation. Eventually sufficient good experiences should consolidate an individual's inner perception of self, and thus a more stable sense of well-being develops as the positive evaluation of others is internalized.

In addition to the companionship provided, a satisfactory friendship with an admired individual enhances the feeling that one is worth having as a friend. In the involvement with another person there is the opportunity to see oneself through that other person's eyes and to find confirmation of one's own goodness. A student, thus, may choose a friend who closely conforms to one's own ideal. Each relationship affords both satisfaction of its own, and a means of measuring the capacity to form a fulfilling bond with another person. With each gratifying relationship, whether the individual consciously notices it or not, the capacity to live with and relate to others increases. Thus, for each person, a friendship experience can help in the further achievement of more mature relationships and to broaden horizons as well as testing and reassuring the individual.

For most students, the first relationship that develops in college is probably an acquaintanceship or a friendship with someone of the same sex. Most dormitory living situations, whether rooming or corridor, are still arranged by sex, and it is only natural that friendships will develop between individuals who are thrown into close contact with each other. Sometimes friendships begin because of participation in a particular activity, which provides not only an initial point of contact but also a common interest:

> Linda had taken up jogging as a junior in high school. She enjoyed the feeling that she was keeping in physical condition and also found that running was an easy way to meet people. All runners seemed to enjoy talking about running, and it was easy to engage in the conversation. For Linda this was a great plus because she had trouble with "small talk" when there seemed to be no common focus. In college she continued to jog and shortly after arriving met a member of the women's cross-country squad who encouraged her to try out for the team. She did so and was pleased to make it. Almost immediately she found that the team

formed a social group that provided companionship away from
the sport as well, and her entire social life became centered around
the individuals on the team.

The choice of friends is not made on the basis of chance alone,
although it is certainly affected by who is available. Friendship
choices are also reflections of who one is at a particular time and
may express who one wants to be, who is admired, or whom one
finds supportive, or who one attracts. The other person's
opinion, or the individual's perception of that opinion, is often
incorporated as one's own. If the perception is not totally
positive, this may lead to insecurity about oneself, but may also
offer some constructive and concrete suggestions for change.
Reassessment of one's personality and behavior may result, a
difficult, a sometimes painful task to accomplish but one that is
often crucial to growth.

If the circle of available people for emulation and identification widens, modifications occur in the initial images of what
one would hope to be like. New possibilities for relationships and
for a changed self-image become acceptable. This process is
partly cognitive but largely emotional, both conscious and
unconscious. It is through new relationships that new identifications, both cognitive and emotional, can be made, and an
enhanced self-image developed in response to contemporary
experiences, which, in turn, may lead to a greater capacity for
commitment and intimacy.

## Formation of friendships

What makes some individuals adept at making friends and others
not? For some, it seems to be a "natural" gift; for others, a painfully learned process, based on trial and error; and still others
never seem to learn. Some people catch the quiet clues from other
people and respond in an adaptive way; others react to the same
clues in ways that alienate. Qualities important in forming friendships are the capacity for genuine interest in the other person, the
ability to be empathic, and the willingness to share, and to

participate. To maintain friendships one needs to be able to compromise, to be flexible, to perceive and respond to the wishes and needs of others. It is important not to be so self-centered as to measure everything in terms of oneself. For more intimate friendships one must be able to tolerate closeness without feeling engulfed. That is, one must have already achieved sufficient separation and individuation to be secure that one is a separate person. These qualities, which will vary at different periods in a student's growth, derive from the student's earlier relationships, particularly the qualities of trust, empathy, and sharing which are related to early parent-child developmental experiences.

Douvan speaks of "interpersonal competence" as "a person's ability to make one's way in the interpersonal world," including the ability to attract others and to form friendships.[31] She also mentions the importance of the willingness to open oneself up and take risks of rejection and hurt. Describing close interpersonal relationships as similar to any creative enterprise, she stresses the ability to accept one's own dependent needs. An important skill is the ability to modulate a relationship so that one does not attempt to become "personal" too soon, on the one hand, or remain "impersonal" too long, on the other. Again, this is not a consciously thought-out process. Its relevance, however, can be understood if one listens to a dialogue between two acquaintances, one of whom lacks this sense of modulation and clearly becomes "intrusive:"

> John and Ed were walking to a class in which they were both enrolled. John asked, "Did you read the assignment?"
>
> Ed answered, "Yes."
>
> John asked, "Did you understand it?"
>
> Ed answered, "Yes."
>
> John persisted and said, "Did you like it?"
>
> Ed again replied briefly, "Not particularly."
>
> John tries again, "I liked the part about England. Have you ever been to England?"
>
> Ed: "No."

It is clear from even this short sample that John is pushing the conversation, Ed is uncommunicative, and John does not respond to his cues. It is not clear, of course, whether Ed does not want to talk to John specifically, whether he simply does not want to talk on this occasion, or whether he is uninterested in the topic. It is probably fair to assume, however, that, if John does not become more sensitive to the indication of Ed's feelings, the friendship is not likely to grow.

The emotional importance of friendship for different individuals varies greatly. For some an eroticized relationship is the only one that really matters, and friendships, although perhaps quite numerous by the individual's definition, carry relatively little emotional investment and may not be especially close. They exist for immediate companionship, because of mutual interests, or because they fulfill some need of the moment. The need may be very limited: for instance, in order to be able to engage in certain kinds of activities such as playing tennis, going camping, or studying. Less is expected of such a relationship, and for some this is a relief. Sometimes limited friendships lead to closer relationships, but they do not need to. Some individuals may have many friends at a given time and place, but if either the individual or friend moves, the friendship terminates. Other individuals will establish friendships that remain viable through time even though the individuals are apart. Often friendships formed at college are the first that will last indefinitely through adulthood since they reflect the adolescent and postadolescent changes in values and "identity."

Some people's usual style is one of isolation, with relatively few contacts other than those absolutely necessary. The underlying psychological basis for this style can vary from being an indication of serious psychopathology to being part of a stable but limited personality style; or it can be the result of defenses developed earlier in life which do not allow the openness necessary for making new relationships. However, patterns vary widely. Sometimes a few crucial people are available to further developmental aims and to serve as models. Although the resulting number of friends may be limited, the relationships are important and sufficient for a given person.

## Friendship difficulties

Destructive, regressive aspects of relationships can also occur. For example, peer pressure can disrupt studying, can involve students in activities in which they would not otherwise engage, such as drug use or drinking or sexual behavior, and from which they may emerge confused and upset. Sometimes this kind of relationship reinforces an individual's low self-esteem:

> Letitia, a sophomore, said:
>
> "I have a funny pattern of friends. Susie has blonde hair, wears great clothes, and can flirt. I feel like a little kid next to her. Gwen is peppy and very funny, a robust kind of kid. I couldn't match her. Nancy's smart and quiet, really efficient about everything. They all seem defined. And I feel like protoplasm.

Sometimes a relationship evokes problems from earlier years. They can strongly affect a student who is vulnerable to criticism, depression, or competition. Instead of being reassuring, experiences with others seem to confirm one's differences and inadequacies, real or imagined. For example, rejection by a valued peer can precipitate a depression. At other times a student primarily lives vicariously through the experiences of friends. Although this seems generally limiting, it may be a path to development, for it offers the possibility of observing new ways and trying them out for oneself in fantasy. When appropriate, the student can actually carry them out at a later stage. Sometimes students are able to "get out of their system" a wish to experiment with dangerous drugs or with antisocial activity by observing the effects on a friend without ever taking the risk themselves:

John entered college with an old high school chum, Jeff. They were both outstanding students who participated in math competitions and chess tournaments in high school but were relatively isolated socially. The college they chose was conducive to a strong group formation, and both became socially involved. John continued to excel academically while Jeff became so immersed in the group that he neglected his studies and began using alcohol and psychedelic drugs heavily. John observed Jeff's behavior. Although he had experimented mildly with drugs, his observation of its destructive effective on Jeff convinced him to give them up. Jeff was forced to leave college and floundered aimlessly for a period of time. Eventually he resumed his studies, but only after a difficult recovery.

In this case, observing the destructive effects of group pressure and heavy alcohol and drug use enabled a student to limit his own explorations in this area, avoid a painful confrontation with reality, and mature through vicarious experience.

Even close friendships are generally not free from ambivalent feelings. The tolerance of ambivalence and the expression and acceptance of aggression are sometimes very difficult for students, and problems with these issues form a large part of student unhappiness. Roommates in particular are the focus of such tension in a college setting when dormitory or apartment conditions limit the flexibility which may be necessary to meet the needs of each. Facing open conflict and handling aggressive expression appropriately may be problematic because it conflicts with an individual's self-concept of being agreeable or nice, on the one hand or runs the risk of alienating a potential friend on the other. Resolution of these issues is an important maturational step. The ambivalent feelings about independence, and the need for privacy and personal space sometimes also provide a source of tension with friends. Negotiations may be difficult because they call upon as yet undeveloped skills and because they may touch upon latent issues with siblings:

Adele had recently moved into an off-campus apartment with four other roommates. She enjoyed the company of the others, having been rather lonely in her dormitory with a roommate who was usually away with her boyfriend. Negotiation about food, cooking, and space were accomplished with some difficulties, but seemed to be working out. She had a room of her own and a shelf in the refrigerator, and enough privacy to study. However, a mounting sense of tension and depression sent her to the counseling center. As she described the living arrangements, she mentioned a cat one of the girls had. The cat was reacting to the move by regressing from being toilet trained to ignoring the cat box and picking obvious places in the apartment to place her deposits. In fact Adele had had to clean up her room more than once and the previous day had had to wash her bedside rug after the cat soiled it. She had talked to the owner, who promised to restrict the cat but hadn't. Adele realized with prodding by the counselor how furious she was. A lifetime pattern of not getting directly angry at anyone supported by powerful values that one should express love rather than anger had made it difficult even to recognize her feelings and particularly to express them. With a great deal of support she was able to confront her roommate who then placed more effective restrictions on the cat. The tension and depression eased, and Adele felt enormously relieved not only to have solved the cat problem but to realize she had not alienated her friend.

Difficulties in forming friendships reflect many levels of personality variations and problems, just as friendships themselves are used for a variety of developmental purposes. The individual may be afraid to risk rejection, or to risk exclusion from a new group, or to expose what are considered unacceptable aspects of the self. There may be lifelong difficulty in trusting others, which is accentuated by a new environment. Problems with individuation, separation, and identity formation can result in anxiety about closeness, because one fears to lose the unstable or fragile sense of self, or to lose control of impulses and feelings.

## Erotic elements in same-sex friendships

Although, as already stated, "friendships" usually describe a relationship that is not erotic, affectionate relationships with persons of the same sex may have an erotic component that is partially conscious; people who are close friends and care about each other may also derive pleasure from some degree of physical closeness (such as touching or hugging). In U.S. society this is quite acceptable between women and is acceptable between men under certain circumstances, e.g., winning moments in sports, or when drinking. However, this does not necessarily (and usually does not) mean that one has an interest in overt genital sexual activity with any person toward whom one feels affectionate. Indeed, the dependable inhibition of such interest may facilitate the safety that people feel when developing strong friendships.

It is possible that a same-sex friendship always includes some unconscious erotic element, but that is not the same as conscious recognition or expression of erotic feelings. Certain current attitudes, however, have complicated the issue. The bisexual nature of humans has been stressed in some psychological writings and by some people who openly state that denying sexual impulses and behavior toward one sex is an undesirable constriction of potential gratification, whatever the individual's preferred sexual orientation may be. Furthermore, there is a current emphasis on "openness" and "self-realization" which, by implication, suggests that if one is aware of feelings, they should be expressed by words or action. Thus, some may define psychological health as the acceptance and gratification of feelings rather than their denial and suppression. Neither alternative, however, is necessarily an "either/or" situation; awareness and acceptance of feelings need not imply their inevitable full gratification. This represents a further choice with complex issues involved. The process of becoming aware of one's erotic feelings and any related conflict and the struggle to resolve the conflicts if they exist and make a choice may be a potential source of maturation and growth as well as a source of stress.

One segment of the women's movement has supported same-sex intimacy by emphasizing the importance of women's support of other women, including a possible anti-male orientation. Some women have been at pains to make clear that this mutual support does not imply a sexual relationship; nevertheless, this possibility is raised by inference, particularly when it is coupled with a warning against becoming dependent on men. Some feminist students take a lesbian position as part of a political ideology and become controlling and intrusive, interfering with the individual's deciding the issue for herself. A woman in such a group can feel caught between her feelings on the one hand and her ideology on the other, and feel disloyal if she is drawn to heterosexual relationships:

> Lisa, a young woman with an interest in literature and a commitment to feminist values, found that a largely lesbian literary group on campus welcomed her warmly. She was pleased to find support on her feminism and literary interest, and felt accepted and secure. By midyear she had become involved with a male student and did not see this as inconsistent. Members of the group did and accused her of disloyalty to her political stance. She felt conflicted that her emotional interests did not "fit" her political position as defined by the group. Moreover, she found it difficult either to leave this otherwise supportive environment or to give up her boyfriend.

In a different context, there has been considerable discussion of the "love" or romantic relationship between men in various popular films. Although these are not always openly sexual, the sexual aspect is not very deeply buried. Thus, some would argue, if intense emotional attachments exist, it would be more "honest" to make them "overt" rather than "covert". Such views creep into the thinking of students who are exposed to and are experimenting with a variety of new relationships. These views create a climate in which more possibilities for expression of these feelings are considered than in the past, and more choices are, therefore, necessary. There is an expressed value favoring being "honest". Such "honesty" may, however, serve many functions, such as a cover for behavior which is either aggressive or self-serving. Some persons "honestly" do not wish to actually engage in certain sexual practices, although they "honestly" may find the idea and the wish to do so acceptable or pleasurable. Accepting or enjoying a wish is different from enacting it. Enactment is a further step and involves some awareness of a wide range of additional aspects of one's self and of the social implications of one's actions.

## Cross-sex friendships

Friendships between men and women have been on the increase. Although the possibility of platonic male-female relationships has always been recognized, usually there has been a presumption that opposite-sex attachments of any strength were usually eroticized and same-sex relationships were not. Thus, the trend toward non-erotic male-female friendships reflects both actual changes in roles as well as the wish of both sexes to be considered as other than "sex objects". As men and women approach equality in a variety of settings, it is important to know how to get along as colleagues and friends. Co-ed dormitories, integrated programs, and the willingness of both men and women to enter new activites have facilitated more friendly contact between the sexes. More cross-sex friendships have developed, and the participants have become aware that they can be comfortable with each other in a non-eroticized relationship. This is expressed in rooming and living arrangements as well, where it is not unusual in off-campus housing for a group to contain male and female students, or even two students, one male and one female, who are not erotically involved with one another and may have boyfriends or girlfriends join the household from time to time in a more flexible way. This may be difficult for parents living elsewhere to understand and accept.

What determines whether a friendship will be sexualized? Rangell quotes Freud as stating that friendship is "aim-inhibited sexuality", meaning that the sexual component of the relationship is not expressed.[32] What determines whether it will remain "aim-inhibited", whether this is under conscious control, and whether the constraints are likely to be dissolved under certain conditions? These are crucial questions in an era when the number of close cross-sex friendships is increasing enormously. If the constraints do dissolve, does it matter? Will the friendship survive as a friendship? These issues all bear on the scope and shape of all friendships but especially on cross-sex friendships, and must also be viewed in the context of societal expectations. The current student emphasis on the importance of cross-sex friendships may be partly a younger generational reaction to what is seen as a disapproving assumption by the older generation that a male-female relationship must be eroticized. This can be translated: "you accuse us of immoral behavior, but it's really you that has the dirty mind—we're just friends." It may also in part be a response to the implication that eroticized male-female relationships are, by traditional definition, unequal with the male, the dominant partner. Thus, the ability to form non-eroticized, cross-sex friendships is an affirmation of the equality of the sexes.

The possibility of platonic cross-sex friendship allows for getting to know well many more people of the opposite sex. Thus, each learns directly about a wider spectrum of people, enabling individuals to learn better what sort of people they do and don't like.

> Althea said: "I was interested in meeting the guys as friends, and it has meant a lot to me. One of the guys in particular, I got very close to as a brother kind of thing. It really is wonderful. He'd come in and talk to me at night about politics because I don't know anything about it, and I'm interested. I talk to him about my latest love life, who I'm going out with. It really meant more to me than I think I know. You know, it gave me a good feeling because I think it's the first time I've ever felt that I was good friends with a guy just on friendship basis."

Learning about people can go on without romantic commitment or erotic involvement:

> Betsy said: "I find myself discussing. . . birth control a lot more with males than I do with females, which is strange. Seemingly the females are the people who should be concerned. I had an argument for an hour and a half in the bathroom with the guy who lives next door to me about abortions. Now you know you just don't talk to women for that period of time about it unless it is to discuss strategy or something. But this was just this incredible thing. He asked me about abortions, and I found myself really trying to let him know what it felt like to be a woman, and to even be afraid to be pregnant, that sort of thing. It's something I just feel. It's something that really comes out of this coed living experience. Both sexes are really trying to make the other sex somehow know how it feels to be that, because we have to share so many experiences. In an all-women's group, things that are really important get skipped over."

For individuals who don't feel ready for an erotic relationship, friendship is a possible first step. For most people, after getting to know several people of the opposite sex well, erotic involvement comes more easily—with a greater sense of choice.

In summary, friendships in the college years are the ground on which most of the other developmental tasks are tested. The growth of autonomy, the process of individuation, the consolidation of sexual identity, the capacity for commitment, and the recognition of the drection one wants to go in relation to intellectual interests and work, all will contribute to establishing satisfying relationship which encourage further ego growth and maturation. In the process there are also periods of regression, with return to old emotional patterns, defenses, and relationships which were helpful or safe in the past. This regression is normal in early adolescence and may occur later as well. However, individuals gradually acquire mastery over situations which at first may be reminders of old dangers and conflicts; in the process they become more mature. In the period of transition from adolescence to early adulthood, the fluidity of movement between regression and progression, as well as the experimentation with feelings, thoughts and relationships, is great. As in other transitional periods, the reworking of earlier experiences permits growth and further differentiation. The process obviously goes on for everyone in this period, but for those in college, the large number of peers, the emphasis on seeking new experiences, and the importance of friendships give prominence to relationships as vehicles of development.

# 5
## LOVE AND SEX

We live in a culture that stresses the satisfactions of love and sex, and we admire those who attain them or proclaim that they do. On all sides, social forms, consumer products, and advertisements sound the siren song that says love and sex is what life is all about. Thus, there is considerable cultural pressure for students to experiment sexually and to fall in love if possible. This pressure is consonant with the physiology of the sexual drives, but may prevail even if spontaneous emotional feelings do not lead in such a direction.

Consequently, most students will develop erotic feelings toward others at some time during their college career. Some fall genuinely in love, some convince themselves they are in love, others know they are not but want to enjoy sex and lose their virginity as a rite of passage, or believe that to "belong" one must be sexually active. Some are not sure what they feel; others wonder whether they are in love, and may restrict themselves to fantasy.

A large part of literature describes the joys and pains of falling in love. Falling in love is usually considered desirable, but popular songs frequently describe the "aches" which are also involved. Love can be an absolutely distracting process, distorting one's perspective and causing irrational behavior. It can bring intense pleasure but, if there is disappointment or rejection, it can be excruciatingly painful, and this can be equally preoccupying, challenging one's self esteem and causing regression and reactivation of old conflicts.

Falling in love and being in love adds an entirely new dimension to most people's experience. The idealization and distortion of the qualities of the loved person have been described. The wonderful sense of enrichment, if the feelings are shared, is eagerly sought by many students. Some feel particularly lonely if they are not involved in a relationship when others around them are, and feel it is a blow to their self-esteem. Although mature love involves recognition of the other person's attributes and the capacity for mutual satisfaction, the initial falling in love may be stimulated by the resemblance of the loved one to an important person, the circumstances, and a variety of other elements which may not necessarily be enduring.

Students may enter college already involved emotionally and experienced sexually, or college may provide the first opportunity for a close sexual relationship. Experimentation as a characteristic of the college period has already been described, and, typically, a series of sexual relationships are explored with varying degrees of intimacy and physical involvement. Gaining the ability to handle the emotions evoked and to remain comfortable is an important developmental achievement of this period and helps further to solidify sexual identity. If intimacy and sexual closeness occur prior to the establishment of a sufficient sense of personal separateness, the intimacy may be experienced as fusion with the partner and provide anxiety. If the sexual relationship occurs without some prior consolidation of a consistent sexual identity, the sexual act may become largely a physical release and offer little in the way of emotional closeness. The relationship of sex and love is of considerable concern for many students, and the formation of standards reflects family values, peer values, and the student's own maturation.

Any relationship, as any particular behavior, may have adaptive functions at the same time that it serves defensive functions. So a relationship with a lover which is protective and dependent also permits the exploration of new dimensions of sexuality and, potentially, commitment. Intimacy in a sexual relationship represents not only the search for a kind of love and caring deriving from early childhood, but also becomes a way of assuming an adult role and expressing feminine or masculine identity. In establishing a sexual relationship, the student furthers the process of differentiation from parents and at the same time identifies with them as sexual people. Not infrequently, although not necessarily consciously, a sexual involvement also raises moral issues, in the form of concerns about the rightness or wrongness of one's actions, and, if these can be resolved, students have come closer to the important accomplishment of constructing their own value system.

The importance of consolidating a gender identity as a developmental task of late adolescence has been stressed. Relationships with an affectionate and sexual component in college form part of this process, although they do not necessarily include sexual intercourse. Feeling attractive and admired offers confirmation of one's masculinity or femininity as well as reassurance of being worthwhile. The sexual relationships of this period are often transitional. Many adolescents have enormous anxiety about their attractiveness, lovableness, and sexual ability, and may be driven to demonstrate repeatedly their ability to be attractive or "make a conquest" in attempts to reassure themselves. If the reassurance ebbs and the process must be repeated, this is an indication that the underlying concerns may be profound. In such cases, psychological help may be required to clarify and resolve the internal doubts and conflicts before a satisfying relationship becomes possible.

## Sexual patterns

There is considerable evidence that a change in sexual values, mores, attitudes, and behavior has occurred in the past two decades. For example, a 1977 study using a sample from all four college years indicated that approximately 78% of the men and 72% of the women had had sexual intercourse by their senior year in contrast to only 50% of the men and women in 1970.[33]

Peer attitudes toward sexuality in nearly all college students are permissive, accepting, and encouraging of sexual involvement. The "double standard" so prevalent in previous decades seems to have given way to a new mode named, by Reiss, "permissiveness with affection".[34] Naturally these changes are not universal. There are some women who cherish their virginity on religious or moral grounds, and there are some who, like Sylvia Plath in *The Bell Jar,* want to discard it as a burden in an almost impersonal, mechanical fashion. More frequently both men and women accept sexuality as a natural part of an emotional relationship, although the sexual intensity and its importance will vary, of course, with the maturational stage and experience of the couple. Although there is much discussion among students about the importance of commitment, in practice many students seem to go through a period of experimental sexual contact that gradually evolves into a pattern of "serial monogamy", i.e., one or more serious and exclusive relationships occurring one after another. A recent study suggests that fidelity seems to occur more than casual sex, although the latter does occur.

Sex is often an area of conflict, and disappointment is not unusual. When this occurs, a period of avoiding all sexual contacts may ensue, followed by subsequent efforts often attempting to discover whether sex has more to offer than the previous experience indicated. Because intercourse is considered the ultimate sexual experience, it is often perceived as a necessary milestone, a hurdle to be overcome, rather than a pleasurable act which is part of a relationship. Thus, the act can be anxiety-producing and actually interfere with development until subordinated to the broader goal of a satisfying relationship.

## College women

Although changes in sexual behavior have occurred for both men and women, the differences seem greater for women. In Western culture, it has long been accepted, even expected, that men will

"sow their wild oats", with the understanding that they would
then be more likely to settle for a monogamous marriage. This
was sometimes explained on biological grounds: namely, that
male behavior is determined, or at least largely influenced, by
hormones and a greater sex drive. Women were thought to be
passive, receptive, and accomodating without a strong sex drive
so that sexual experimentation was unnecessary. Current views
question this difference and hold that sexual behavior is not
solely biological but is also an expression of cultural
expectations. Women have not been free to acknowledge their
sexual wishes because to do so was considered "loose" and
"immoral". Furthermore, until recently women had little control
over pregnancy so that sexual experimentation carried the risk of
very real consequences. Women's sexual responses vary, but
women are now understood to be as interested in the sexual
aspect of a relationship as men. Differences in interest and excitability between men and women have been described by Kinsey,
et al., who present evidence that the peak of male interest and
excitability is in late adolescence and early adulthood, i.e., the
college period, while for women it is later in life.[35] However,
those studies and their findings may have been influenced by the
social constraints on women's sexual freedom which may have
allowed women to be openly sexual only at a later maturational
stage.

In Victorian times free expression of sexuality in middle-class
women was clearly forbidden and criticized. It is still regarded
ambivalently by older and more conservative segments of the
population. However, today, many young women enjoy their
sexuality, initiate it freely, and have multiple partners with seem-
ingly little conflict. In fact, as was indicated earlier, the prior
pattern has been modified, in that by senior year almost as many
women have had intercourse as men,[36] and some studies have
shown that women have a higher incidence of intercourse.[37]
Furthermore, the frequency of intercourse is higher for women,
and women currently engaged in a greater variety of sexual

patterns. Women entering college may form casual relationships with or without sporadic short-lived sexual experiences; one or more sexual encounters may occur with several partners with varying degrees of pleasure, guilt and anxiety; or sexual contact may form part of many relationships or of just one or two which then may develop into more sustained relationships. Men obviously also engage in casual sex, but their patterns seem less varied.

Some students may happily accept the traditional woman's role and look forward to marriage at the termination of college.[38] This pattern tends to occur more often in conservative and religious schools. These students identify with and continue to accept their parents' traditional values. If there is no internal questioning of the values at any time, the student may be evidencing a failure to establish an independent identity, but these attitudes do not necessarily represent a lack of individuation; it is one of the possible routes of development. These same students may deviate markedly from their parents' values in other areas.

Students who come from traditional backgrounds and make a determined effort to lose their virginity may be using sexual activity as an expression of rebellion against parental values, pursuing in part another route to emotional separation:

Priscilla, the older daughter of a small town Southern lawyer, fell in love with a student who was of another religion. She was a highly idealistic and ambitious young woman who believed in total honesty and truth. During a Sunday morning telephone conversation with her parents, she announced to them her new involvement, and told her mother that she had entered into a sexual relationship with this man. Mother was horrified. She told Priscilla that she was no daughter of hers, advised her to break off the relationship and return home. She was angry and disapproving. Priscilla was equally indignant and horrified. She accused the mother of being antediluvian, of not living up to her liberal injunctions that all men are equal, and refused to budge from school. Father stepped in between the two angry women, trying to mediate and keep the peace.

Eventually the parents came to a business meeting close to the University, and her mother reluctantly agreed to meet the young man. Priscilla brought him and a cordial and pleasant evening ensued. Priscilla and her mother began to speak to each other cautiously, and during this exchange, both began to understand each other's point of view. Since Priscilla's grades continued to be excellent, she was allowed to remain at the University. Mother reluctantly agreed that the young man was appealing and gave her blessing to the relationship. Somehow, after peace was made, the patient's interest in her lover diminished. Eventually she broke off her relationship with him.

In retrospect it became apparent that Priscilla's strong attachment to her boyfriend was fanned by the mother's opposition. At least part of the need to tell her mother of her sexuality was an attempt to gain acceptance and sanction from her mother for her new role as an adult woman. When her mother refused to give such sanction and wanted to keep Priscilla in a dependent, childish position, she became angry, and stubbornly attached to her lover. Her feelings about the relationship intensified beyond the point that they would have if the attachment had not also fulfilled a function in relation to her mother.

The internal ties to the parents are still strong, but establishing contact with peers helps to break them. The sexual relationship thus may serve several purposes simultaneously.

The shifting societal standards have permitted students a greater overt expression of sexual wishes with acceptance by the college peer community. However, internal conflicts may be created by the differences between current standards and previously internalized prohibitions and judgments:

Constance had sexual relations with a number of relatively casual dates, because she thought she and her date wanted and expected it. Each time the sex seemed to fit into the relationship easily. Slowly, however, she began to worry when openness and acceptance of sexuality stopped and promiscuity began. Although her external behavior gave the impression that she had resolved the problem, internally and to a great extent unconsciously, she was troubled.

The threat or appearance of a venereal disease can mobilize this conflict into conscious expression:

> Alice vacationed at a resort where she had a brief pleasant sexual relationship with another vacationer. Both saw this as temporary, and she regarded it rather more casually than he. Returning home, she resumed a pattern of occasional sexual friendships with several men.
>
> She seemed untroubled by the pattern until the man she had met on vacation told her that he thought he had gonorrhea. She felt upset, but nevertheless told her various lovers and with apparent mastery of the situation sought medical help. She was treated for a chronic vaginitis which eventually turned out not to be gonorrhea. She had been distressed at the idea of having to tell her lovers that she might have transmitted the disease, but had not waited for the diagnosis to be confirmed. She was relieved to find out that it was not gonorrhea. That night she dreamt that she returned to the doctor, who shook his head gravely and said that her clitoris would have to be cut off. She awoke in a panic, realizing that her guilt about the gonorrhea was an expression of previously unrecognized conflict and guilt regarding her sexual behavior.

## College men

Changes in sexual patterns for college men suggest that men attach greater importance today to a full and satisfying emotional relationship rather than "simply having sex" as seemed prevalent previously. Men on a "macho trip" who brag loudly about sexual conquests are less obvious in college today. There seems to be less focus on "scoring" and more preoccupation with sexual performance, success in pleasing partners, and a fear of sexual inadequacy. At a health center one hears more frequent concerns about sexual performance, such as premature ejaculation, secondary impotence, and retarded ejaculation. Some men are trying to free themselves from their earlier more rigid traditional stereotyped male roles.

Some male students will still embark on a period of sexual experimentation with many casual sexual contacts and engage in a competition with other men in an effort to be considered the campus Casanova. Conversely, some are shy, fearful of women, and preoccupied with studying, leaving little time for socializing. Shyness for these students may represent a reaction to their projected fears of women, who are perceived as dangerous and hostile. Gradually new images and experiences can change their perceptions.

As has been mentioned, changing social values leave the student with much of the responsibility of setting his or her own sexual standards, which are influenced by peer behavior and expectations as well as by earlier family experiences. There is frequent conflict and anxiety, such as that experienced by Constance in the vignette above who became concerned about promiscuity. The process of determining one's standards is usually maturing. For a very few, sufficient anxiety will emerge so that there is a premature closing off of options and a relatively rigid resolution of conflict that does not portend a very happy sexual future. For the majority, the task of working out an acceptable and fulfilling code of sexual behavior and response is accomplished satisfactorily.

# 6
## LIVING TOGETHER

The extent to which unmarried couples are openly living together represents an enormous shift in social behavior from that of a generation ago. From Victorian times until very recently male/female love and sexual relationships, at least in the middle class, were conducted by a generally agreed-upon set of customs. Everyone recognized that these customs were modified on occasion and were different for different cultural and social class groups, but they remained the rules of the game. Courtship for middle class young adults was a relatively well-regulated series of steps, from dating to engagement and marriage. No longer is this necessarily the course of true romance. Even in earlier times, matters did not always proceed so smoothly, but there was a clearer pattern of expectation. According to popular belief, the woman coyly played a carefully orchestrated game of "unavailability" while surreptitiously arranging to lure the unsuspecting man into a proposal of marriage. On his side the man was actively pursuing the woman, while simultaneously attempting to preserve his bachelorhood. Although this description usually applied to general courting relationships, there was a specific sexual parallel in which the man was seen as aggressive and panting for sexual intimacy while the woman was demure and protective of her presumed innocence, and more precisely of her virginity. This model was based on several promises: that all males would push for intercourse; that women were interested in marriage, not sex; that nonvirgins would be spurned as marriage partners; and that birth control measures were uncertain and pregnancy might occur. Needless to say, there was some truth in several of these premises, but the full truth was considerably more complex.

It is clear that much has changed. Although the great majority still say they hope to be married some day, marriage for college women as well as men is by no means the only goal. Furthermore, the new "arrangement" of living together even as undergraduates has been introduced as a viable possibility, one which until recently was largely done secretly or restricted to a self-styled avant-garde group.

In the 1920s many prominent thinkers, such as Bertrand Russell and August Strindberg, actively promoted living together on the theory that such a trial would reduce the number of marriages in which the partners were found to be incompatible after the fact. Judge Ben Lindsey most articulately advanced this idea in his book, *Companionate Marriage*.[39] The idea, however, never really caught on, probably because of the climate of public opinion which found it unacceptable, although the difficulty of controlling pregnancy may also have been a factor. It should be emphasized, moreover, that when living together came to be a more generally accepted pattern in the 1960s, it was not then, nor is it today, in any sense necessarily thought of as a trial for marriage.

Currently, living together represents an often ambiguous relationship in which the ground rules, boundaries, styles, and goals differ widely from couple to couple, and often are neither examined nor articulated. Some couples have established a relationship akin to a nonlegalized marriage; others run the gamut from housing convenience to intense but transient emotional involvement. If, as has previously been postulated, commitment cannot contribute to maturation without sufficient sense of self, then it can be understood that for some this arrangement is a basis for growth, whereas for others it is confusing and a source of anxiety. It may even serve a defensive function, interfering with exploration and with the development of sexual identity, although the existence of sexual contact when viewed externally seems to be furthering this very process. Anxiety may occur particularly when the shape of the relationship is not explicitly addressed, leaving many expectations unexpressed and providing few conventions to serve as guides. It is essentially a new pattern, pioneered, as is usually the case, by the younger generation, with acceptance by the older generation often still an issue. Thus, the younger generation may find it difficult publicly to admit problems associated with living together for fear of losing ground in the fight for attaining its acceptability. At the same time, older generation members (other than those who simply condemn it) feel that any attempt by them to raise questions inevitably labels them as moralistic and reactionary. While some older couples are "living together" for their own reasons, they may be critical of, or concerned by what their children are doing. Many young people are themselves judgmental or anxious about the idea, but will only acknowledge their feelings in a confidential setting, such as that provided by psychotherapy.

Most undergraduates are not emotionally or financially ready for permanent long-term commitments, but they are trying to discover who they are and whom they care most about and relate to best. Relationships that are inflexible make this process difficult, and most college relationships will turn out not to be permanent. Patterns of living together may emerge casually, sometimes almost accidentally and often partly determined by dormitory architecture and rules under which undergraduates live. For example, college regulations usually preclude two students of the opposite sex from officially sharing a dorm room, so that often couples, who may have a strong sexual and/or emotional attachment, will maintain, at least officially, separate living quarters. This may delay "real" commitment or provide a safety valve if things become difficult or if the relationship dissolves. Those colleges, however, in which many students live off campus are less likely by their policies to influence or modify the students' range of options.

Although some students are reluctant to give up some

"outside" sexual activities on their own part and are willing to tolerate some on their partner's part, most hope at least temporarily for a committed monogamous relationship in which the couple can become really close and intimate both physically and emotionally. Such relationships sometimes develop between two young people quite easily and spontaneously without much obvious soul searching, while others will spend much time analyzing their own feelings and those of their partners before being willing or able to commit themselves even transiently.

The individual meanings of living together vary considerably, and, as with other relationships, represent different cultural and developmental issues. If the couple maintains separate addresses, the living together may start casually with one member staying over for the night and repeating this process until both are spending most of their time in the same living space. In this situation there may be no binding commitment and not even much discussion. A decision to live together more completely by giving up separate living quarters requires an element of trust and willingness to surrender one's private space and to relinquish an "escape hatch". This represents a serious step for many young couples and sometimes involves giving up the protection of the other roommates or dorm-mates. Because there is no formal contract, formal commitment is in a sense always left open although emotional commitment may be intense. Some couples look on their relationship as equivalent to marriage. For the latter the decision not to marry may be a lack of belief in the concept of legalized marriage, or it may simply mean that they feel marriage is an unnecessary formality, especially if children are not planned. However, even if the arrangement is clearly not "permanent" and the couple has not thought of marriage, or preserves a we'll-see-what-happens attitude, the issue of commitment inevitably looms in the background if not the foreground. These issues become more prominent after the undergraduate phase.

Some welcome the lack of formal commitment and feel that

the lack of a binding agreement creates a less "tied-down" feeling, and that the lack of obligation to maintain the relationship tends to de-fuse situations that are potentially explosive. The couple may feel that the openness also means a constant and important affirmation of the relationship. Others feel that in any prolonged relationship there are going to be periods of acute tension, and that a legal marriage which is not so easily dissolved acts as a deterrent to impulsive action and as a positive spur to working things out. These two viewpoints can be further elaborated with one point of view stating that it makes no sense for two people who are not happy living together to stay together simply because they once participated in a marriage ceremony, and the other stating that without some commitment of an indefinite nature the temptation to solve problems by breaking up will be very strong.

For many couples who live together, problems and tensions arise after an initial period of fulfillment. Some may be minor and occur when joint purchases are contemplated or when social invitations come to one or the other member of the couple. If, however, one or the other partner begins to feel that the relationship is somehow taking on more serious implications, the problems may be more complex. These feelings may result from conscious or unconscious demands that one partner makes on the other, or because one or the other is not able to tolerate the intimacy or the commitment. There may be external reasons, i.e., a pregnancy that precipitates examination of the relationship and the need for choices; or one partner may have a greater need for permanence or commitment forcing into the open the need to make decisions which have been avoided up to that point. Then all sorts of ambiguities, misunderstandings, or unexpressed feelings come to light. The result may be difficulties or further maturation.

Jealousy can be an issue, whether or not there is explicit commitment to an exclusive arrangement. Neither partner may be prepared for jealous feelings, nor for the imposed expectations of the other. They may have reached an agreement in which relationships with others are permitted, or this issue may never have been openly confronted. But jealousy is often not prevented by even apparently mutual agreement. It has its roots in developmental experiences, for instance, in relationships with siblings, rivalry with parents, or in a need to be the exclusive partner. This need may be especially strong at this time when the student is attempting to develop a self-concept as someone who has the ability to sustain a relationship. In a more open, less committed relationship, the expectation that there will be others in the partner's life may be clearer, and this expectation helps to deal with some of the anger, disappointment, rejection, and jealousy, but certainly does not entirely eliminate it. Furthermore, students often may expect themselves not to feel jealous if they have consciously arranged for a more "open" relationship and, when they do, they may feel more upset by the fact that they feel jealous than by the jealousy itself because they feel such a feeling is "abnormal", or inconsistent with stated ideals.

Money and property frequently present difficulties to a couple living together. This, of course, does not necessarily distinguish living together from marriage, but some of the ground rules are less clear. In marriage, there have been certain conventions and responsibilities, and while many of these are currently changing, at least the married couple tend to consider themselves a unit, with some expectations of supporting themselves together. When two people live together, the financial arrangements may be ambiguous, and this may lead to resentments and tensions. Ways of handling money can create considerable disagreements because of different backgrounds, styles, and individual meanings of money, but can also be a way of symbolizing problems about expectations and sex roles.

If partners who live together break up because both wish to, there is little problem. If the breakup is engineered by one member, as it usually is, the other one may have a very difficult adjustment. It never has been easy for a lover who has been left, but in this situation the rejected partner may not only adapt to the emotional loss but also to many accomodations in living. Because the living-together relationship has not carried the premise of permanence as does marriage, there is very little social support for those feelings of outrage, hurt, and anger, which are considered "justified" when a marriage breaks up, nor any particular formal provision for dealing with feelings of loss, loneliness, and failure. Divorce may be—and often is—a very unpleasant process, but the disentanglement necessary around common property and the formality of the proceeding provides a framework for expressing feelings and receiving support. When people living together break up, there is often a feeling of void and considerable generalized depression for which they may receive very little sympathy.

For the person who has difficulty making long-term commitments for unconscious psychological reasons, living together may provide a socially acceptable way of life which is highly adaptive as long as neither member of the couple wants children. Some individuals feel that a series of successive relationships has positive advantages; for example, in exploring different aspects of their own personality. Such individuals might go through life quite successfully moving from relationship to relationship as long as new ones are available, never being forced to face the fact that they have a problem with making a full commitment to a given relationship. This may of course be difficuly for their partner to tolerate. However ideal an arrangement living together may seem to be from a student's viewpoint, when both partners are doing more or less equivalent things and are in a period of experimentation and change, this perspective can change with graduation. Then decisions about jobs or graduate school make remaining together a more conscious choice which requires more planning, and the issues involved in commitment resurface.

Social acceptability and parental attitudes may also represent problems. Even those parents who may easily tolerate their son or daughter living with someone while at college or in a distant city may have a different view when the couple arrive home. Then separate bedrooms may be assigned plus admonitions not to tell grandmother, or aunts, or uncles, which reflect the parents' mixed feelings of tentative acceptance and disapproval. This inevitably seems silly and hypocritical to the couple, and considerable friction may develop as a result. Some parents are accepting but confused as to how to handle social conventions, and tensions may arise out of awkwardness. Some parents can accept living with one partner because it seems to approximate marriage, but having a consecutive series of partners may be less acceptable and lead to disapproval or bewilderment.

One part of this reaction may be the manifestation of an attitude gap between the generations in regard to marriage, career, and children. The parental generation, at least in the middle class, tends to have been brought up in an era which believed that marriage was certainly a goal for every daughter, and probably for sons also. A premarital affair for a young woman was not only condemned on moral grounds, but also supposedly decreased marriageability. Although under the double standard a young man was expected to have premarital sexual experience, parents worried that a sexual involvement might trap him into an indesirable marriage. Some of these attitudes probably remain even though the realities have changed. Thus, for the parents, the living-together arrangement involved not only the immediate issue of morality but also the whole question of their child's future.

An important additional aspect is the parents' confrontation with and their reactions to their offspring's manifest sexuality. This may be a particularly sensitive area because it often occurs when the parents' own sexuality may be undergoing the changes of mid or later life. Complex reactions develop within the parents as their own maturational issues are revived, stirring up their own sexual anxiety or making them feel older, i.e., more identified with their own parents. Simultaneously, for the undergraduate, because the relationship often takes place in the context of the still uncompleted task of separation, each close, interdependent, and sexualized relationship may represent a displacement of an expression of unresolved, unconscious ties to parents.

For the couple, even though the relationship may eventually dissolve, the experience of living together may provide longer term developmental gains in addition to the immediate satisfactions of companionship and sexual stability. First, the everyday realities of sharing the tasks of living make for a more realistic view of marriage in contrast to the traditional courtship routine which provides an inaccurate preview of the actualities of married life. This statement once might have related primarily to the sexual side of marriage; now, however, a greater degree of mutual sexual experience is likely to have occurred prior to marriage, but the equally important nonsexual aspects of marriage may be largely unknown. When an individual has experienced a period of living with someone, many of these aspects such as food patterns, capacity to compromise, sleep and waking cycles become clearer although, obviously, living with each given individual will be a different experience. Living together in a house shared with others can be a transitional stage in commitment. One is paired with another, but in a family-like context, with some needs met by the other housemates.

Living together can evoke aspects of parents' marriages, sometimes with unconsciously motivated repetitions. The degree of commitment, sharing, necessity for compromise, and the necessity to consider someone else's needs can call up unresolved internal problems which may have been hidden earlier:

> Steve had no difficulty finding women who were interesting and attractive to him. He would spend a great deal of time with them, share vacations, and feel a closeness and intimacy. However, the moment he made a move to change the relationship to one of living together—even though they still maintained separate living quarters—he would become anxious and intolerant. He would recall his parents' poor marriage and separation, and his mother's

possessive and intrusive demands on him. (He had dealt with these in early adolescence by literally leaving his house and staying with friends, or by involvement in school and athletics.) Then, the current relationship would seem suffocating and overwhelming.

Once he panicked when a girlfriend hung some of her clothes in his closet. At another time, on returning to school from a camping trip late at night, he insisted that his girlfriend return to her own apartment even though this meant traveling some distance. When he developed a relationship with someone he cared about greatly, and they did try to live together, he found that she began to seem less attractive to him, and their sexual relationship deteriorated. He realized this was a manifestation of his anxiety about commitment, but the relationship was severed anyway. Eventually he sought professional help for this recurring problem.

Since ambiguity is a frequent component of life situations, a couple may gain from learning to tolerate the anxiety that may result. In this way, living together can also act as a significant learning experience on an emotional as well as a day-to-day "getting along" level. However, if the level of anxiety created by the ambiguity or by other aspects of the relationship is too high, the individual runs the risk of experiencing inhibition rather than growth, because protective defenses are mobilized to cope with anxiety. These range from withdrawal and unwillingness to risk a future relationship, at least for a while, to more severe kinds of emotional reaction. If the anxiety can be mastered, the way may be opened to richer and more fulfilling relationships.

Living together is an increasingly prevalent pattern among students, which, depending on definition, may be somewhat less frequent than one might suppose from reading the public media, but which clearly has grown in popularity on college campuses over the last decade. This growth has been sufficient so that those who do live together are essentially indistinguishable in demographic characteristics from those who do not. In describing reactions to the experience, some students felt that the rules and norms were not as rigid as for marriage; others had sought an intimate "love" relationship that was less permanent than marriage; and many did not plan to marry. In one study by Macklin at Cornell, reasons given for cohabitation included "loneliness of a larger university; the superficiality of 'the dating game'; the search for more meaningful relations with others; the emotional satisfaction of living and sleeping with someone who cares about you; the desire to try out a relationship before considering marriage; and the widespread doubts about the very institution of marriage."[40] The author notes, however, that the decision to live together was rarely a purposeful act based upon careful reasoning and planning.

# 7
## HOMOSEXUAL RELATIONSHIPS

In the college years many students have some homosexual fantasies, feelings, impulses, or experiences, and some students seriously question their sexual orientation. This may be the expression of aspects of a person's identity, or represent experimentation
which involves trying out homosexual relationships as well as
heterosexual ones. Misconceptions about homosexuality still
abound. For instance, some continue to believe that having some
homosexual experiences or feelings or even a single experience
means that someone *is* "a homosexual".

Affectionate or warm feelings toward someone of the same sex
may be mistaken for sexual feelings. Even the recognition of
sexual feeling toward someone of the same sex does not necessarily mean that individuals must define themselves as "homosexual". These feelings may be subordinate to heterosexual
feelings, which represent the dominant sexual orientation.

Although most people have both affectionate and sexual
feelings toward both men and women at one time or another, the
various factors determining one's primary sexual orientation are
complex. Sexual orientation is a very sensitive area, particularly
for men who are often concerned about masculinity and feel that
any hint of homosexual feeling is a threat to their maleness.
Consequently, many have difficulty if they find themselves
feeling warmly toward or liking other men. If the feelings are
clearly sexual, they may have difficulty integrating these feelings
with the concept of themselves as men. The struggle with homosexual feelings can at times block developmental progress.

Some overt homosexual activity may have a positive function because it allows the individual to test the fantasy in reality which may help to clarify the strength or persistence of the wish and perhaps its function, e.g., a homosexual experience can clarify whether this is or is not what the student wants. For some individuals there does not seem to be much choice about sexual responses, but there may be choice in their expression and how one chooses to conduct one's sexual life. The wish for a close relationship with a person of the same sex may repeat the unconscious aspect of the relationship with same-sex parent or sibling, or the search for an idealized self. Once the underlying issues are made clearer, individuals then decide consciously whether they are or are not interested in such a relationship. Some people may find it useful to seek help in clarifying these underlying issues by talking with a psychotherapist.

Many erotically-tinged attachments between individuals of the same sex never become actively sexual, and the erotic element may be more or less recognized or acknowledged by one or both partners. They may exist between roommates, or be represented by the crushes that girls have on older teachers or on peers, or more clandestinely by the admiration males often have for athletic stars. They may also exist when a student has strong sexual desires for a friend who is clearly heterosexually-oriented. Some, as was mentioned earlier, are acted out because of group support or even pressure. Many or most are transient. However, some students come to college with an established homosexual orientation; others will discover a homosexual preference during college. This may be accepted smoothly or accompanied by feelings of distress at being "different," a feeling which is reinforced by general parental and social disapproval of homosexual orientation.

Some of the real difficulty students feel stems from the confusion that exists in both the public media and the scientific literature about the origins, normality, and mutability (or immutability) of sexual preference. This confusion is not helped by the frequent moral and religious statements that are made on

the subject so that it is not surprising to find that many young
men and women feel battered by conflicting ideas, by uncertainty
about their own sexual impulses, by concern about what these
impulses portend if they are other than conventionally
heterosexual.

The struggles of one man with these issues are illustrated by
the following account of someone looking back on his college
years:

> Simon said that his first homosexual contact was at the age of
> twelve and from that first encounter throughout high school there
> were repeated encounters. He goes on to talk about his experiences:
>
> In spite of that, I refused to consider myself homosexual. I knew
> I had little desire for women and as my peers each found their own
> heterosexuality, I became aware of a widening gulf between them
> and me. My reading told me that homosexual desires and even
> manifestations were not uncommon in puberty—I seized on that
> and convinced myself that I was simply a little late in making the
> transition. I went off to college fully expecting, like Saul on the
> road to Damascus, to be struck down by heterosexuality. It did not
> happen in my freshman year. That year, however, I was pre-
> occupied with my new environment, my new freedom, and the
> adaptation to collegiate life. However, my choice of friends that
> year was among those who led virtually no man-woman social
> life.
>
> In my sophomore year, I decided that if heterosexuality wasn't
> going to find me, I was going to have to find it. That was what
> prompted me to join a fraternity.
>
> Here too the gulf between my peers and myself was obvious—in
> fact, overwhelmingly so. I debated about retreating several times,
> though I didn't. I decided that I had homosexual tendencies
> indeed, although I still didn't consider myself a homosexual. As a
> result I became celibate. But not for long.
>
> While out of college for a year I had my first, last, and only
> intimate heterosexual encounter. The only way I could consum-

mate the affair was to fantasize about a man while "doing it" with a woman. That left me really mixed up as I felt I had just negated my identity hypothesis. This was followed the next summer (after graduation) by an incredible affair with a fellow fraternity member who was not homosexual before and after the summer we spent together. I came away from that summer having experienced my first real love affair with anybody—one that was reciprocated in every respect. I remember the joy and serenity it gave me—and I also remember that I drew all sorts of comparisons with the affair before, all to the effect that I would love to spend the rest of my life with this man and I cared not a whit about the woman. But in all of this, neither he nor I talked about being "homosexual" nor identifying ourselves or each other as one. It was very much a "happening". When we terminated the affair we both decided that being homosexual would be incompatible with our other goals. For me, that became my operative policy—as well as more celibacy. I again refused to consider myself homosexual—now because I didn't practice. That lasted through graduate school and on through my career until finally I couldn't hold the tiger in chains any longer and I began a process of self-analysis and self-acceptance which culminated in my "coming out" three years or so ago.

In spite of the "victories" of that summer, I do not consider myself to have "integrated" my personality and achieved a workable level of self-esteem and self-confidence until the coming out—that was the last big piece in the puzzle of me.

I want to emphasize the overwhelming importance that the issue of self-acceptance played in my college years. It was *THE* problem which preoccupied me. School work was an escape from the problem. Until the resolution of the self-confidence business, studies were an escape from that too.

Things might be easier now for a person in my predicament. There is more acceptance by others and more understanding of the troubles of later teenager/early adult. But I sense there is still a problem in understanding people like me (not necessarily homosexual) and the conflicts which were tearing me apart. And I don't think I'm at all unique.

Homosexual relationships for college students include many of the same rewards and difficulties as heterosexual relationships, but, in addition, they pose some problems that are different. As has already been stated, general acceptance of homosexual activity and homosexual relationships has increased in the last decade, especially among groups, such as college students, that have a live-and-let-live attitude toward peer behavior. In spite of this, many students do remain critical. The greater acceptance as well as the more open demonstrativeness of the participants has led to increased visibility for such relationships, which, in turn, sometimes evokes more active expression of the intolerance that other individuals and groups continue to have toward homosexual behavior. Furthermore, the lack of legal machinery to formalize a homosexual relationship inevitably creates greater uncertainty around commitment and permanence. The present political debates about the civil rights of homosexuality-oriented individuals tend to polarize the issue and at times to create a certain self-consciousness in those individuals openly engaged in a homosexual relationship. People in heterosexual relationships do not usually have to cope with these added difficulties.

It is important to distinguish between those students who have been clear almost from the beginning of sexual awareness that their only sexual interest is either heterosexual or homosexual and those individuals who, for whatever reason, have been aware of some sexual feelings for both sexes although they may lean predominantly toward one or the other. One must also distinguish between homosexuality as a phase in the experimentation and exploration of relationships, homosexuality as a defense against heterosexual involvement, and homosexuality as an orientation which is expected to be permanent. However, during the college years even when a choice is apparently permanent, change can occur as a consequence of internal change and growth, or external experiences.

Students with a definitely established homosexual orientation would be well advised to choose a college which is openly tolerant to gays. Even in a tolerant college, a student may wish to establish a homosexual relationship and find it difficult to meet someone because potential partners are rather guarded about their preferences. For those seeking to establish stable homosexual relationships, there are special problems relating to acknowledging sexual orientation, which, if announced, may restrict the opportunity to meet a variety of people and affect potential maturing experiences. Furthermore, the shifting nature of relationships may leave the student vulnerable to jealousy, feelings of betrayal, and desertion. Since the college period is a time of change, one partner may shift sexual orientation while the other does not. The lack of social norms of behavior to deal with such problems may create considerable discomfort and confusion for both.

In some ways homosexual couples currently have many problems in common with living-together couples. In both, the sense of commitment may be a crucial issue; the roles in the relationship taken by each member of the couple are less based on clear-cut tradition; and issues of family acceptance may be a major factor in how the relationship develops. Furthermore, in both there may be subtle or not-so-subtle disapproval from the "outside" world, ranging from landlords to neighbors. The homosexual couple, however, is more likely to run into gratuitous disapproval or even abuse from acquaintances or groups of students who know of the relationship only by hearsay, an unlikely happening in the case of a heterosexual couple. Social acceptance facilitates such relationships and removes some of the external strains, but internal conflicts about overt behavior still may exist for both, although they presently would be more likely to be found in the homosexual couple. Of course, these would probably have been equally intense for heterosexual couples not too long ago, so that the situation may change for homosexual couples in time.

Another important aspect of the homosexually-oriented individual or couple is related to the campus social milieu. Since the advent of "gays" as an overt and public minority group, there has been a tendency for gay students to form a social group which may not interact very much with other campus groups and, thus, a measure of isolation results. This has an effect both on students who are, or wish to be, members of the group and on students who may be quite clear about their homosexual preference but are worried about announcing it for social as well as psychological reasons. Once announced, they may feel social pressure to affiliate with the gay world which may or may not be the social milieu they prefer at college. Conversely, although heterosexually-oriented students may accept the gay individuals' sexual preference, they may make certain assumptions about their preferred social activity and not include them in an activity that has a heterosexual setting. Students who are uncertain have particular difficulty since joining a gay group may constitute more of a commitment than they intend because of the tendency of these groups to isolate themselves, which in turn causes a greater dependency on the gay social group. Thus, students can be locked into a social milieu which hinders flexible exploration and development in other areas. However, gay groups have gone a long way toward raising the self-esteem of their members, which, as has been noted, is an important developmental task in college for everyone, but may be particularly important for the homosexually-oriented individual who has traditionally been subject to low self-esteem.

Although the foregoing discussion addresses some of the problems and confusions that currently exist in society related to homosexual orientation, it is clear that homosexual relationships can reach high levels of emotional and sexual gratification, and for many students the college period represents a time when there can be an inner acceptance of homosexual feelings and an opportunity for fulfillment in a relatively congenial environment. For many who come from the more conventional "heterosexual" high school world of male football heroes and female cheerleaders, college represents the first social milieu in which a number of people can be found who have common interests of a nonsexual nature as well as possibly a similar sexual orientation. Living arrangements are conducive to developing such relationships since in college same-sex individuals are expected to live together. Social arrangements are usually informal; thus, showing up for a party with an individual of the same sex, if thought about at all by others, might be interpreted as inability to get a "date". Since students expect to support themselves, money issues are not likely to arise, and there may be relatively few external strains on the relationship. Thus, the college period and environment may be a particularly happy and unstressful time for a homosexual relationship, if both partners are resolved in their choice.

The joys and sorrows of heterosexual relationships have been dealt with in foregoing sections. Homosexual relationships have the same potential joys and sorrows, but are different in a variety of ways. They are subject to greater risk of societal and parental disapproval, as indicated earlier. Statistically, stable relationships seem more difficult to maintain. The reasons are not as yet clear. For some, there is the additional issue of whether this is a permanent life choice or a transient phase, an issue that occasionally arises also with heterosexual relationships but is less likely to do so.

# 8

# RELATIONSHIP DIFFICULTIES

Although, as has been stated in several of the preceding sections, relationships are essential for development, it is also true that difficulties in the course of relationships can lead to unhappiness and at times may have disastrous consequences. The subject of relationships cannot be covered without some consideration of these. Here we are not addressing difficulties individuals have in forming relationships because of problems of trust, intimacy, commitment, and other maturational difficulties.

For some the problems may lie in an inability to form relationships without considerable stress. If, in the effort to be gregarious, an individual resorts to alcohol or drugs, the outcome may have grave consequences. The student may do this in order to feel less inhibited and, therefore, better able to communicate, or because entry into a group in which drinking or drug-taking is a major social activity is perceived by the student to require one's engaging in the same activity in order to belong, to be "one of the gang". If the individual then comes to believe that drinking is necessary to establish sociability, or is susceptible to addiction, there may be longterm consequences that are secondary to the physiologic effects of substance use.

In a somewhat different vein, there may be serious effects of unrequited love or of love relationships that break up. Rejection may be especially difficult in a developmental stage when self-esteem is highly important, when one's sexual identity may be shaky, and when one is attempting to individuate from the family. The rejected individual may react primarily to the narcissistic injury involved rather than the loss of the specific lover, but the pain is no less for that fact. Deep depression may ensue and many, if not most, of the suicide attempts made on campus occur after such a rejection. The suicidal behavior may express depression at the loss, anger at the lover for having left, and greatly lowered self-esteem. The situation may have been made particularly painful because the rejecting lover remains in the environment and seeing the person at meals, classes, and extracurricular activities may be a constant reminder of the breakup. The two individuals may even be a part of the same friendship group, and the rejected individual has the difficult option of regularly seeing the old lover or finding new friends. Occasionally, the rejected lover, especially if a male, will resort to violence in an attempt to reestablish the relationship or, failing that, to injure the woman.

The ways in which people cope with rejection may also have adverse consequences. The phenomenon of the "rebound" relationship is well known. Although such a relationship may work, it may also break up if its basis is not very sound, leaving the individual even more convinced of being unable to manage a close relationship. Turning to alcohol or drugs may be resorted to as a means of "forgetting". Women often feel that the relationship would not have ended if they had been more physically attractive, which in today's fashion means thinner, and a bout of anorexia may ensue. Another possibility is that the felt inner emptiness may lead to overeating and excessive weight gain. Furthermore, the student may withdraw and essentially avoid any close relationships for a time. If the time is not too long, this may serve as a period for regrouping and consolidation of psychological resources. If it goes on indefinitely, however, it may become a hindrance to further development by making the individual too wary to risk new relationships of any kind.

# 9
## RELATIONSHIPS WITH OTHER ADULTS

Most day-to-day experiences and relationships in the college setting are with peers. Although this is what most students expect and anticipate, for some there is too much homogeneity in a steady diet of such relationships that the presence of older faculty and staff and the opportunity to establish friendships with them can leaven. Thus, faculty and advisors are important to students not only as teachers of subject matter, but also as people with whom students can have relationships which foster personal development and provide insight into varying adult life styles. Since they are more distant than family, the tensions of evolving separateness are more diluted and less likely to be played out with faculty and staff members. However, faculty and staff may indeed occupy parental roles, and feelings about parents or siblings may be displaced onto teachers, deans, dormitory personnel, or any other adult who is felt to be in a position of power or authority. The student may perceive the adult as if he or she were indeed the parent, and bring to that relationship feelings and responses which derive from the past relationship with the parents and, therefore, are inappropriate for the present.

Faculty and staff may also respond on the basis of their own past rather than to the real issues presented by the student. Irrational prejudices, dislikes, attachments, anxieties, and distortions can complicate these interactions. It is important for these to be sorted out:

Paul, a sophomore, moved into a new dorm. He also joined a choral goup. The leader, a young faculty member, seemed to him to be critical of everything he did. Paul felt he was working hard but no matter what he did he could not earn a warm response from the leader. He began to doubt his ability and to wonder whether he should remain in the group. One day, he overheard the instructor describing to someone the three or four students he felt were absolutely dependable and could be relied on to learn their parts, attend rehearsals and do their best, and he was one of the students mentioned. He was astonished, relieved, and elated. He realized he had mistaken the leader's reserve for a critical manner, similar to his own perfectionistic, grudging father. This enlightening experience made it possible for Paul to reexamine the old relationship, his tendency to perpetuate it inaccurately in the present, and to possibly move beyond to a new more realistic position in relation to authority figures.

Personal contact with older people has many implications for the development of students. Everyone has some ideas about what being an adult is, which qualities are admirable or possible, and which are not. These notions start within the family, and are gradually expanded as the person is exposed to more people. In addition to the opportunity to enlarge this experience with contemporaries, college offers the chance to observe and get to know some older individuals whose backgrounds, interests, and ways of life may be very different from those of the student's. The student can observe these variations in someone who is at a later point in development. Some of the decisions the student may be considering are actually lived out by the faculty or staff member. For a receptive student, observing and perhaps participating in new modes of behavior can open up new, hitherto unconsidered possibilities of interests of life styles and for some, these new relationships will radically alter the direction of their lives. Thus, many students find role models within the faculty for deciding how they wish to shape their lives. At times these role models become over-idealized, thus serving the student's psychological need to separate from earlier relationships but at the same time to re-attach to form new identifications.

Sometimes a relationship with a faculty or staff member becomes a sexual one. Most frequently a female student becomes involved with an older male teacher. The young woman student is particularly vulnerable to the interest of an older man who is endowed with authority and is romanticized, and who may arouse feelings relating to her idealized feelings about her father. Although sometimes such relationships have evolved into lasting, mutually rewarding ones, an eroticized relationship with a faculty member often impedes development of autonomy and independence for the student. For the student to feel entirely safe with older individuals who also assume parental roles, there has to be some assurance that sexual feelings will not be acted on, because the student may have unconscious sexual wishes toward family members and is frequently relying on relationships with faculty to help move away from the eroticized family relationships. If the faculty member is seductive or responds to the romanticized attitudes or even flirtation of a student by initiating an explicit sexual relationship, this relationship carries risks. For a relationship of this sort between faculty member and student to work out, both need a level of maturity and capacity for mutuality which is unusual.

Some faculty-student sexual relationships are more clearly exploitative. Sometimes the faculty member may apply overt pressure. When this is accompanied by power implications— overt or covert—such as a promise of a grade or influence, it may become sexual harassment, and some institutions have established procedures to deal with such actions. Conversely, the relationship may also be subtly, or not so subtly, initiated by the student for reasons of advancement or gain derived from having an influential faculty member as a friend. Although this probably happens more frequently with graduate students, it may on occasion involve undergraduates. It is probably accurate to state that no sexual relationship that is exploitative is beneficial to the exploited partner, but it may be especially damaging to a student who is still experimenting sexually and who is attempting to sort out earlier more dependent emotional ties from more mature and adult love relationships. Although the following example involves a female student and a male faculty member, homosexual relationships can also follow similar patterns:

> Lois, a 27-year-old single female graduate student, developed a severe depression and inability to work on her thesis and came to the health center for counseling. She was on the last stretch of her work, having completed her course work with honors, and had chosen a topic but not yet written her dissertation. She had tried to prepare an outline for her advisor who was due to return in the fall. Her despondency was such that she could neither sleep, nor read for any length of time. She felt restless, irritable and tearful, and shunned the company of her friends. She was a large, articulate, and unhappy woman. It became evident that the depression was related to the return of her advisor, with whom she had been involved sexually until shortly before his departure when their relationship was terminated. The advisor felt unable to leave his wife and child whom the patient saw as a manipulative woman who used her weakness and recurrent depressions as a means of holding on to the professor. Lois greatly idealized the professor who was described as a magnificent, witty, and brilliant, internationally known scholar.
>
> The patient was an only child, born in America shortly after her parents emigrated from Europe. Her father was admitted to a mental hospital, though the nature of his illness was never clearly defined.
>
> Lois was approximately six years old at the time of her father's hospitalization, which was considered a shameful event and never discussed in the family. She was raised by her mother and an aunt who ran a grocery store. She does not remember her father whom she only saw once or twice before his death when she was twelve years of age. Mother never remarried, and raised the patient to mistrust men, encouraging her to concentrate on her studies, so as to be able to be completely independent and self-sufficient. When

the aunt's boyfriend swindled mother and aunt of their savings, the lesson of men's perfidy was reinforced.

In the early course of therapy it became clear that the patient's feeling for the professor were related to her past feelings toward her father whom she saw as a martyr, and whom she both missed and was angry at. She saw the professor in a similar light, as being mistreated and bound by a suffering, sick woman. Her original fantasy involved being the favorite student "daughter" of the professor. Yet, once they became lovers, he left her, thus repeating the desertion of father, and fitting in with the picture of men who use women, then leave them. When she became aware of her anger at the professor and her fantasies of revenge, such as exposing him, abusing him, not showing up for her appointments, she suddenly became aware that not writing the thesis was a form of revenge—his star pupil not getting her Ph.D.! This insight was followed by a lifting of her depression, lessening of conscious fear of the professor's return but still inability to become actively involved in her work. It was necessary first to work through the issue of her tendency to overidealize and overglorify relationships. She tended to get deeply involved with her women friends, and expected almost immediate intimacy and mutual caring. This rarely matched her friends' expectations and resulted in recurrent disappointments. In a sense it was also true of her relationship with the professor because she actually knew before she became involved with him that he had been divorced three times and had a reputation as a womanizer. He enjoyed humiliating students and had a sadistic streak thoroughly evident in his interaction with his wife that Lois had observed during numerous departmental parties. She became aware of her anger and disappointment in her girlfriends, in her mother and in her aunt. She then had a brief relationship with another older man, during which she finally discovered that her professor was a very inadequate sexual partner, and that the sexual relationship had been very disappointing to her, though she was not able to admit it to herself until she experienced a different approach. She found out how much she idealized him and how she tended to blame herself and her presumed lack of sexual attractiveness for the shortcomings of the sexual relationship. Only at this point was she able to resume her work and meet her professor without losing self-control. She was able to refuse his attempts to resume the sexual relationship and turned to other professors in the department for help with her thesis work which she completed successfully.

Faculty relationships perform one further function in the current rapidly changing world. Because faculty and staff are exposed to many young people they are often more familiar with and reasonably tolerant of new life styles, and they can often bring a more balanced viewpoint toward experimenting with and exploring these life styles than other adults can. Consequently, students may be helped to articulate their feelings and attitudes and to learn more from their own experiences than they might otherwise. Younger faculty who are themselves struggling with issues about sex roles and life styles can also be very helpful. For example, faculty and staff who are personally involved in working out ways of handling dual career marriages or family relationships with or without children may be interested and willing to discuss these issues and their feelings about them with students. Such faculty will act partly as role models, and partly as consciousness-raisers introducing new possibilities. Competitive feelings may arise, either spurring or interfering with the constructive value of such relationships. When these occur, they, too, often reflect and repeat dynamics of the early family constellations of both student and counselor, but because the relationships tend to be less intense than with the family, they may be easier to keep in perspective and, perhaps, resolve.

Relationships with family, faculty, counselors and other adults often change quickly, reflecting the fluctuations in development of the student, who may feel more independent at one moment and less mature at the next. For example, at one point a student may genuinely ask a resident tutor, advisor, or faculty member for specific advice about a concrete problem and immediately thereafter decide that one should make up one's own mind at all costs and reject out of hand the requested and carefully thought-out advice. The tutor may feel insulted or, more sensitively, realize the student's conflict between seeking guidance and wishing to be independent. Understanding this conflict can help the advisor to maintain objectivity and be more tolerant toward behavior which might otherwise feel like a rejection. For young faculty who may still be partially in or just beyond the same developmental phase as their advisees, this insight may be especially important, because they are only beginning to resolve some of the same issues themselves.

Everyone brings his past experiences and expectations to new situations and relationships. Advisors and tutors are no exceptions. If the advisor has been brought up to consider certain behaviors acceptable and others outrageous, the adivsor's personal reaction is predictable if a student's behavior falls into one or another of these categories.

The judgment of advisors may even be clouded by irrational prejudice, and the more advisors can understand their own predilections, preferences, and dislikes, the less likely they will be to impose them inappropriately on adivsees, and the freer advisors will be to help the students develop their own personality, style, and interests.

Faculty members and advisors may have other reasons for idiosyncratic responses to students. Students may represent part of the faculty members' sense of themselves as young adults, and, thus, the faculty member may be living out part of their own past rather than responding directly to the problems that the students present. Students provide a vehicle for faculty members to work out their own difficulties. Students, however, are searching for relationships with older individuals who are genuinely interested in them, and, if this aim is undermined by faculty members' own needs, students will inevitably feel disappointed or confused. It is not necessary, however, for advisors and faculty to mask their own preferences and values for some attempt at "objectivity". In fact, a clear statement of one's own values, while accepting the student's differences, can be an integrating experience for the student. But faculty members must have a genuine investment in the relationship and not "use" students for essentially self-centered goals. This is facilitated by the faculty member's awareness of his/her own goals and needs as compared to the student's.

# 10

## THE COLLEGE ENVIRONMENT

The college environment provides an opportunity for students to suspend adult social roles and responsibilities while pursuing scholastic and vocational goals. Thus, college differs from the working world of young adults who have to support themselves, or from the world of those who live in countries where the period of adolescence is not so prolonged. This is true even if the student is commuting to college and lives at home. The college milieu allows exploration in the cognitive, personal, and social spheres. The importance of relationships is usually not explicitly stressed, yet, whether acknowledged or not, is a crucial part of the curriculum. The proximity of many people at all times of the day and night with the freedom and time for interaction, the possibility of bull sessions lasting into the morning, the myriad opportunities for chance meetings on and off campus, the shared experiences and problems, the common interests of people of the same ages and the camaraderie and democracy of the campus make the college situation an especially privileged one. Many an intellectual, literary, or political movement has had its origin in college residence halls because of the freedom to explore new ideas and to try out new identities.

Colleges vary considerably in the environments and services they provide that enable students to learn and practice necessary adult tasks. There are environments including libraries, laboratories, museums, and athletic facilities. There are extracurricular activities, part-time job opportunities, and there may be some organized health care facilities. The latter may include a mental health service and a sex education, contraception, and problem pregnancy counseling component within a health center. There may be counseling services with opportunities for self-actualization, participation in personal development groups, and a career advisory service. While learning how to take advantage of any or all of these services and facilities, and how to organize their time, students are preparing to manage in the wider communities and life situations to come.

Changes in college environments in the last few years reflect changes in society at large. The liberalization of sexual mores has been accompanied by a shift in the college administration's attitudes toward the social and sexual behavior of students, with a continuous movement away from the "in loco parentis" role of previous years. Co-residential living is part of this recent trend, as is the elimination of many of the parietal rules of the past. These changes make it possible for students to experience a wider range of relationships and behaviors. With this freedom, and in the absence of rules, as we have indicated, responsibility rests more with individual students to set their own limits while exploring possibilities and potentials. Students may have the choice of a variety of living arrangements—on-campus residence halls, fraternities/sororities, in-town apartments, which may also be mixed sex with friends who do not become lovers—or they may remain at home. Day-to-day living arrangements have an enormous influence on the quality of a student's overall experience.

Relationships are fostered by comfortable proximity. Most dormitories provide this. Most studies show that friendships form and flourish between people who have easy access to each other— usually by living nearby in dormitories. Thus, living on or near campus is important in fostering a variety of relationships and in feeling part of the college community. The architectural arrangement of space is critical. Many small rooms in highrise dorms can be isolating, and lack of space devoted to comfortable socializing can have the same effect. Sometimes, constant proximity to others may be felt as too intense. Because of noise and other interferences a dormitory room may be inconvenient for studying or sleeping. Privacy is sacrificed. A more insecure or less assertive roommate may be at a disadvantage and suffer through a difficult semester. When such a situation comes to the attention of the residence hall staff, they may attempt to help the at-odds roommates to reassess their situations, personal values, and degrees of assertiveness, so that the differences can be modified, and living conditions made more tolerable. In extreme cases, one or both of the students may be allowed to change rooms. Although this may be trying, the students often benefit from the negotiation process.

Situations where groups of students spend significant periods of time together foster a wide range of relationships. Certain extracurricular activities, particularly athletics, but also activities such as the school paper, theatre, and music groups, besides teaching a skill, serve this function. Officers, representatives to student government, social, and athletic chairmen need to be elected; intramural teams to be chosen and practices scheduled; decisions on "House rules", visitation policies, and use of collected social funds to be decided upon. These events are repeated each year with successive groups of students providing roles for almost everybody and an opportunity for self-definition and enhancement of self-esteem.

For commuting students and those who live off campus, the absence of adequate provisions for contacts outside the structured classroom situation may have a profound effect on the development of friendships and involvement in the overall college experience:

> Billy, a junior at his state college, lived in an apartment with a high school classmate. Together they spent most of the week studying. Billy would look forward to seeing Sally, a 16-year-old girl he had been dating exclusively for three years, and he and his roommate would leave early Friday afternoon and drive the two hours to their isolated home town in the mountains. At the end of

the spring break Sally suggested that they start dating other people, and on successive weekends couldn't spend time with Billy because of "other plans". He sought professional help because of increasing difficulty with sleep and an inability to concentrate on his studies or in class.

Fraternities and sororities and some other small living units afford the opportunity of acquaintance with a broad range of peers, but in a smaller, more homogeneous group. The "brothers" and "sisters" constitute "family" away from home and help ease the separation from parents. They may also provide a more gradual opportunity to reconsider parental values and develop autonomy; this, in contrast to the shock of meeting fellow students with totally different values, which may too suddenly question the basis of a student's pre-college world. However, as with other close groups, there is the possibility that strong allegiances may inhibit the cultivation of friends outside the group, or promote an exclusivity that isolates "outsiders" and encourages complacency within the group thereby reducing exploration. The tighter the group the greater the likelihood of informal ranking of people and hierarchical arrangements of worth, of set expectations of performance, and of norms that when violated may lead to ostracism and in themselves be inhibiting to experimentation and growth.

There are other subtle aspects of the campus climate that significantly affect attitudes. For example, in a setting of considerable freedom for young healthy individuals, sexual pressure can be intense and can lead to the use of force. Rape of one student by another does occur, and often authorities have looked the other way and not confronted the violation of autonomy and choice which is involved. If the incident is seen as understandable "wild oats" on the part of the man, or if it is felt that the woman should be able to maintain control and, consequently, "must have been acquiescent", or "led him on", the true stresses and crises are not confronted and the student who has been the victim may not receive help with a real trauma. How colleges and universities react to such crises will influence students' perceptions of cultural attitudes and male-female relationships. In addition, many campuses are in urban areas in communities with high crime rates, and students are vulnerable to attack from outside the college. These experiences can be so upsetting and disorganizing that either the student or the family insists on withdrawal from school. Sexual harassment or rape can provoke embarrassment and guilt that the student cannot discuss it, and, as a consequence, suffers silently, and may develop difficulties with long-term relationships. Efforts that the college makes to prevent such attacks and to offer support when they occur may counteract a potentially damaging experience. An effective and available counseling service or a college-based rape prevention center can be crucial in lessening the damaging effects of such a trauma. Openness to confronting these experiences and to following through is extremely important.

College administrators should bear in mind that the ambience of the college and the opportunity for informal interaction and socializing is vitally important to the student in the overall college experience. It is important to create a climate for acceptance of relationships, both physical and social, and to establish a setting in which comfortable, easy interchange is possible, and help is available when difficulties arise. Relationships during these formative years are enriching in themselves, and are crucial to each student's personal development. Time and money devoted by the university to facilitating such relationships will be very beneficial to students.

# 11
## TRANSITION FROM COLLEGE

Rates and patterns of development vary tremendously among people. Most of this report applies to all college periods. It is difficult to pinpoint patterns which belong to specific college periods because different students go through different phases or crises at varying points in their college careers. However, as in freshman year when everyone grapples with problems of entry into college, the senior year again presents all its members with the same challenges: leaving college and deciding what to do and where to go next. Feelings about leaving college can be poignant and reawaken some of the same feelings of leaving home. As in freshman year, these feelings may affect the strength of relationships in a way that does not necessarily contribute to development. Decisions must be made that include serious consideration of what one wants most for oneself alone, and for others with whom one has relationships. As in leaving home, some of the conflicts of leaving a familiar environment may recur.

If there is a serious lover, the relationship needs to be reviewed in a new light. Problems that immediately arise are the career plans of each partner, the anticipated geographic location of each, the financial situation, attitudes of parents, and even attitudes of peers. Furthermore, seniors are at an age when marriage is culturally approved and may be economically possible, which adds another dimension to the choices. Along with these more or less practical problems, there are internal issues such as uncertainty about increasing the level of commitment and, perhaps even more important, the decision to close off other options. Thus, each partner is pressured to wonder whether the other is really "the one", and, if they separate geographically, to wonder whether he or she will run the risk of losing out. If, however, he or she is not quite sure that the other is "the one", will a commitment at this point be premature? The transition also can offer the possibility of leaving a relationship which has been or becomes regressive, inhibiting, or otherwise replete with conflict:

> Joan and Ed had drifted into living together in their senior year after some months of a sexual relationship. Joan was fascinated by Ed's differentness from her family. Instead of their ambitious, work-oriented, and striving style, he was easygoing, sloppy to the point of defiance, interested in art and experimental films, and politically radical. He wasn't sure whether he wanted to make films, paint, or go to law school. It seemed that he was going to take some time off after college to make up his mind. Joan wanted to proceed to graduate school. She also found that some of her fascination with Ed's interests and living patterns turned to irritation after awhile when he continued to be indecisive. Their sexual relationship deteriorated and they began to bicker. However, she felt dependent on him, and unwilling to think of negotiating the familiar world of campus without him. As graduation approached she felt relieved. She made plans to go to a graduate school at some distance. Ed got a job on campus. Moving into a new situation had its problems for Joan but facilitated her leaving a relationship she no longer found gratifying.

If both students are contemplating careers that involve graduate school, the issue is complicated by the fact that applications must be submitted at the latest by the winter of the senior year, and because most graduate schools have rolling admissions, decisions may be required at a different time for each partner. Questions of compromise then arise if one partner accepts a school that is not his or her first choice (in order to insure being close to a partner) and then later receives a place at a preferred school. The problem of graduate school may also raise, for the first time, issues involving roles and expectations. Some males may be quite comfortable in an egalitarian relationship until the issue of career surfaces. Then, the male may automatically assume that any compromise that must be made will, of course, be made by the female. If she does not accept this assumption the entire relationship may be thrown into question.

Paradoxically, parental opinion about a relationship may become more important in the post-college years even though the fact that the partners are closer to adult status would suggest the opposite. While the individuals are in college, parents may not particularly favor the relationship or a living-together arrangement if one exists, but they may essentially choose to ignore it. With graduate school, however, issues of financial support may arise, and parents who are not committed to support a student through graduate study may be able to use finances as leverage. Although many graduate students are totally self-supporting, compromises may be necessary to attain that state, and, again, issues of compromise may create conflict in the relationship. For example, one partner may need to work or one school may offer more financial aid but be less desirable, and the decision to accept the more desirable school may be influenced by the availability of other sources of funds.

Parents may also apply psychological pressure because they feel a living-together situation after college has different implications than one at college. This may be in part because it is more public. It is one matter to be able to say that Joe and Jane are "going around" together at college, leaving it rather vague as to what they are actually doing, and quite another to explain that Jane is moving to the wilderness because her friend, Joe, has a job there. Furthermore, parents may feel that marriage prior to completing college is undesirable, but marriage after college is very desirable so if Jane wants to be with Joe, why are they not getting married? Although, in theory, Jane and Joe have reached adult status and should be able to make decisions for themselves, their attachment to parents may still be important, and parental opinion may remain an important pressure, with one or both individuals unwilling to defy it.

Peer pressure, also, may be a factor. Marriage is not so important a source of conflict with career as is having a baby, so the current dilemma revolves less around marriage itself but more in the plans that the couple may have for children. The woman may suddenly and unexpectedly discover that the man visualizes marriage as implying a child as soon as possible regardless of the impact on her career plans. A slightly different version of this problem is illustrated by the following example:

> Beth was a senior, applying to law school. Her boyfrield Jim and she were lucky to be accepted by law schools in the same city.
>
> While in law school they lived together and shared cooking, housekeeping, and friends, and supported each other through exams. At the end of law school they decided to get married.
>
> Beth was offered a job in a corporate law firm. She enjoyed the challenge of the theoretical and practical problems, and also the contacts with people. Jim worked as an assistant to a legislator. There was a fluctuating pace to his work, with intense activity at times when the legislature was in session or at campaign times, with slower periods in between. When he had some time off he wanted to take a ski trip. Beth was unable to arrange the same time off. He was indignant—having never realized that he expected to set the pace of their lives together—in spite of the give and take of student days.
>
> Beth felt in conflict. Her mother had always helped her father with his social life and accomodated to his vacations; she felt guilty and disloyal.
>
> When their first baby was born she obtained maternity leave of two months. Her firm was reluctant to extend it, and felt that it would not be feasible to have her work part-time.

> For a while Jim could spend a fair amount of time with their baby. Then his work demands increased. Beth felt conflict between their ideals and plans and the actual dilemma that they had to resolve. Jim felt proud of Beth's job but angry that he could not have the support and flexibility he felt his father had had. How to set the priorities? Whose work was more important? How can compromises be worked out?

The significant fact in the resolution of most of these problems is that psychological work is involved. The necessity for commitment, the necessity for compromise, the decision to break up a relationship, or the assumption of a more independent status in disagreeing with parental or peer opinion all require inner resources and shifts in the prior psychodynamic balance. These shifts all contribute to psychological development, in that they are conflicts that most people must deal with at some time in their adult life. The ability to do so constructively, and without a degree of turmoil that is disruptive to adequate functioning, is an important psychological measure of maturing. The psychological work involved represents a further step in the development of an individuated person. Most students will to some degree have to face these issues during college. Doing so on leaving college is different because they seem more "for keeps", more real. Thus, each individual has to confront the issues more directly and to make decisions which are more often definite and lasting than formerly.

# 12
## CONCLUSION

In spite of the major social changes which have occurred in patterns of relationships during late adolescence and young adulthood, the underlying developmental tasks that each individual must face and resolve in the path toward maturity remain unchanged. Although the forms of expression of friendships and the variety of sexual and social patterns may seem different from those in the past, there are still fundamental similarities in the internal processes. The latter involves the achievement of a balance between separation, individuation, and autonomy, on the one hand, and relatedness, commitment, and the attainment of the capacity for intimacy, on the other. The consolidation of each individual's identity is an ongoing maturational process which occurs during this period. Social changes may have profoundly affected and do affect the world that today's students live in and their options, but it is important to recognize these underlying developmental issues and not to be diverted by more immediate phenomena from understanding them.

Relationships form the matrix in which the developmental process takes place. They are an extremely important part of the college experience. Students may at times fluctuate in their concentration on the courses and the academic aspects of the educational process, which may give rise to concern, but in attempting to assess this, it is important to consider these other aspects of the student's life, i.e., relationships, the learning from others which constantly takes place, and the interaction between

116

cognitive and emotional growth. One may understandably worry if a student is insufficiently involved academically, but the importance of the student's emotional life must be recognized.

During the college years, the student has the need and opportunity for experimentation in relationships as well as in courses. The quality and type of these relationships are closely connected with the student's state of development; each affects the other. There is no ideal path nor a single timetable which is right for everyone, but a variety of pathways, combinations, and directions. There is a wide range of relationships—from acquaintances and close friends to lovers and sexual relationships—which are important in developing the capacity for intimacy.

It is desirable that students have the opportunity for many sorts of relationships and that they are able to have some choice in order to fulfill a range of needs and to gain different experiences. In the absence of adequate models from the older generation, students use each other as models, and peers can come to have a special influence. In part, relationships with peers reflect old family relationships, often with attempts at new resolutions. Adults, such as faculty, counselors, or administrators can serve a special function as substitutes for family, but in a new context which may further the process of individuation and identity formation. Some students may need help with these tasks. The stresses may be sufficiently unsettling so that symptoms appear which interfere with functioning and ongoing development, and professional counseling may be indicated.

In the current period of economic austerity and concern with the cognitive goal of education, it is essential that all concerned with the college experience—students, faculty, staff, and parents—recognize the closely related goal of emotional growth. Support and facilitation of both are a crucial part of the total educational process.

# REFERENCES

1. Sigmund Freud. Three Essays on Sexuality (1905) in the Standard Edition. Vol. VII (London: Hogarth Press, 1953), pp. 125-245.

2. _____ . Some Psychological Consequences of the Anatomical Distinction Between the Sexes. Standard Edition. Vol. XIX (London: Hogarth Press, 1961), p. 243.

3. Jessie Bernard. THE FUTURE OF MARRIAGE (New York: Bantam Books, 1973).

4. National Center for Health Statistics. *Monthly Vital Statistics Report* 31 (8).

5. Lawrence Kohlberg and Carol Gilligan. The Adolescent as a Philosopher. The Discovery of the Self in a Post Conventional World, *Daedalus,* Fall 1971, pp. 1051-1086.

6. William G. Perry. FORMS OF INTELLECTUAL AND ETHICAL DEVELOPMENT IN THE COLLEGE YEARS (New York: Holt, Rinehart & Winston, 1968).

7. Sigmund Freud. NEW INTRODUCTORY LECTURES OF PSYCHO-ANALYSIS (1933) (Lectures XXIX-XXXV) Vol. XXII (London: Hogarth Press, 1964, pp. 1-183.

8. Erik H. Erikson. CHILDHOOD AND SOCIETY (New York: W.W. Norton, 1950).

9. Anna Freud. THE EGO AND MECHANISMS OF DEFENSE (New York: International Universities Press, 1946).

10. Peter Blos. ON ADOLESCENCE: A PSYCHOANALYTIC INTERPRETATION (New York: Free Press, 1962).

11. Margaret Mahler, Fred Pine and Anni Bergman. THE PSYCHOLOGICAL BIRTH OF THE HUMAN INFANT (New York: Basic Books, 1977).

12. Heinz Kohut. THE RESTORATION OF THE SELF (New York: International Universities Press, 1977).

13. Peter Blos. THE ADOLESCENT PASSAGE (New York: International Universities Press, 1979).

14. See citation 11.

15. Carol Gilligan. In a Different Voice: Women's Conception of the Self and Morality, *Harvard Educational Review* 4:4 (1978).

16. See citation 11.

17. See citation 8.

18. Sigmund Freud. The Dissolution of the Oedipus Complex. Standard Edition. Vol. XIX (London: Hogarth Press, 1961), p. 173.

19. John Money and Anke A. Erhardt. MAN & WOMEN, BOY & GIRL (Baltimore: Johns Hopkins University Press, 1972).

20. See citation 8.

21. Erik H. Erikson. IDENTITY AND THE LIFE CYCLE (New York: W.W. Norton, 1980).

22. J.M. Tanner. Sequence, Tempo and Individual Variation in the Growth and Development of Boys and Girls, Aged 12-16, *Daedalus*, Fall, 1971.

23. See citation 13.

24. See citation 13.

25. See citation 6.

26. See citation 11.

27. See citation 6.

28. See citation 19.

29. Elizabeth Douvan. INTERPERSONAL COMPETENCE: THE CAPACITY FOR INTIMACY [in press].

30. Webster's THIRD NEW INTERNATIONAL DICTIONARY (Springfield, MA.: G. & C. Merriam Co., 1966).

31. See citation 29.

32. Leo Rangell. On Friendship, *Journal of the American Psychoanalytic Association* 11 (1963) 3-55.

33. Joseph Katz and Denise Cronin. Sexuality and College Life, *Change* 12:2 (1980) 4-49.

34. Ira L. Reiss. THE SOCIAL CONTEXT OF PREMARITAL SEXUAL PERMISSIVENESS (New York: Holt, Rinehart & Winston, 1967).

35. Alfred C. Kinsey, Wardell B. Pomeroy, Clyde E. Martin and Paul E. Gebhard. SEXUAL BEHAVIOR IN THE HUMAN MALE (Philadelphia: W.B. Saunders, 1953).

36. Ben B. Lindsey. COMPANIONATE MARRIAGE (New York: Boni & Liveright, 1927).

37. Eleanor D. Macklin. "Review of Research on Nonmarital Cohabitation in the United States." In EXPLORING INTIMATE LIFE STYLES, Bernard L. Murstein, Ed. (New York: Springer, 1978). Chapter 9, pp. 197-244.

38. See citation 37.

39. See citation 36.

40. See citation 37.